Become a Healthy Homemaker

Rupa Chatterjee

Published by:

F-2/16, Ansari road, Daryaganj, New Delhi-110002
☎ 23240026, 23240027 • *Fax:* 011-23240028
Email: info@vspublishers.com • *Website:* www.vspublishers.com

Regional Office : Hyderabad
5-1-707/1, Brij Bhawan (Beside Central Bank of India Lane)
Bank Street, Koti, Hyderabad - 500 095
☎ 040-24737290
E-mail: vspublishershyd@gmail.com

Branch Office : Mumbai
Jaywant Industrial Estate, 1st Floor–108, Tardeo Road
Opposite Sobo Central Mall, Mumbai – 400 034
☎ 022-23510736
E-mail: vspublishersmum@gmail.com

Follow us on:

© Copyright: V&S PUBLISHERS
Edition 2018

DISCLAIMER

While every attempt has been made to provide accurate and timely information in this book, neither the author nor the publisher assumes any responsibility for errors, unintended omissions or commissions detected therein. The author and publisher makes no representation or warranty with respect to the comprehensiveness or completeness of the contents provided.

All matters included have been simplified under professional guidance for general information only, without any warranty for applicability on an individual. Any mention of an organization or a website in the book, by way of citation or as a source of additional information, doesn't imply the endorsement of the content either by the author or the publisher. It is possible that websites cited may have changed or removed between the time of editing and publishing the book.

Results from using the expert opinion in this book will be totally dependent on individual circumstances and factors beyond the control of the author and the publisher.

It makes sense to elicit advice from well informed sources before implementing the ideas given in the book. The reader assumes full responsibility for the consequences arising out from reading this book.

For proper guidance, it is advisable to read the book under the watchful eyes of parents/guardian. The buyer of this book assumes all responsibility for the use of given materials and information.

The copyright of the entire content of this book rests with the author/publisher. Any infringement/transmission of the cover design, text or illustrations, in any form, by any means, by any entity will invite legal action and be responsible for consequences thereon.

Printed at Repro Knowledgecast Limited, Thane

Contents

Preface 5

1. Health & Nutrition 7-31
The Weather and Health 9
Food, Dieting, Anorexia and Bulimia 11
Exercise and Good Health 11
Health Check-Ups 14
Investigations 16
Good Health and Water 17
Constipation 19
How Yoga Fights Stress 20
Breathing Correctly 21
Sleep and Sleeping Disorders 21
Sleep Well-Hazards to Our Health 22
Hazards to Our Health from Pollution 23
Health Effects 26
Food and Nutrition 27
Storing Food 27
How to Buy Medicines Over the Counter .. 29
Menu Making for Daily Meals 29
Menu Making for a Party/ Party Cooking ... 30
Health Watch 30

2. First Aid 32-52
Work, Emotions and Mental Health 32
Caring for the Sick 33
Alternative Therapy 34
Home Remedies 35
First Aid 41
Shock 42
Asphyxia 43
Colour Therapy 49
Food Poisoning 49
Foods that Will Fight Cancer 50
Water 51

3. Personal Grooming 53-74
Exercise 53
Calories 53
Massage 56
Good Posture 57
Skin Care 58
Facial 59
Hair 62
Make-up 66
Clothes and Jewellery 71
Know Your Body Type 72
Fashion and You 74
Colour Aesthetics and You 76
Men 76
Summer Clothes 77
Chiffon 80
Jewellery 82

■ ■

Preface

Management has become a key element of modern life. Whether in office or factories, commercial businesses or the hotel industry, systems have been developed to ensure the smooth and efficient functioning of any organization. Since this is so, why should the home which is the first and primary unit of organization be left behind? There is a need to organize the home front so that we are able to function efficiently when we step outside its doors.

For centuries, the role played by the homemaker—wife, mother and housewife has not been adequately appreciated. This job receives no monetary remuneration, there are no prescribed working hours and often the housewife downplays her role by saying, "I am just a housewife". This is a sad spillover from the success-driven, money chasing Western norms that are invading our society. In keeping society healthy, happy, well-nourished and balanced, the home manager and home management plays a pivotal role, since she is called upon to be a chef, a financial wizard, an interior decorator, a doctor, a nurse, a psychologist, a wife, mother, daughter-in-law, friend and social worker—all rolled into one!

I strongly believe that the homemaker/housewife plays an invaluable role. For example, the child or teenager who is given nutritious and lovingly prepared food at home, will not be forced to live on a diet of fast food which leads to obesity and also malnutrition on account of the empty calories present in the food. In fact, Dr. Jyoti Sharma in an article entitled "Straight To His Stomach" published in the September 2000 issue of *"Woman's Era"* magazine goes so far as to say, "What ails Western society is lack of cooking skills" as she noticed that in Frankfurt, Germany, ..."women do not cook there. They survive on canned food, or they buy fast food."

I hope this book will be of practical use to both young girls who are expecting to set up house which is helthy looking for the first aid knowledge, trying to make their home 'happy' as well as to experienced homemakers who may also find some of the information innovative. I also hope that this volume will bring a greater understanding and respect for the many hours of continuous hard work that goes into the running of a well-managed household.

—*Rupa Chatterjee*
July 1, 2001

CHAPTER-1

Health & Nutrition

Life today has become very demanding. Juggling the pressures of the work place along with responsibilities of the house poses an enormous strain on us. In the process we tend to neglect our bodies. Blood pressure and diabetes are just some of the common ailments which are a result of this high pressured life style.

Although cases of polio, leprosy, typhoid, cholera and tetanus have gone down in India, HIV/ AIDS, malaria, asthma, cancer, tuberculosis are on the rise. While the concept of "Health For All" is undoubtedly a laudable goal, our efforts to achieve it have not been totally successful. While painstaking research by medical doctors and scientists have helped to develop new techniques and products in surgery, pharmacy and social and preventive medicines, our lifestyles and the polluted atmosphere in which we live have given rise to new diseases. The stresses and strains of fast-paced modern living has brought in its wake attendant medical and physical problems. In addition, there is a wide range of psychosomatic stress related diseases and not even children are exempt from these traumas. A World Bank and Harvard University report says that depression is set to sweep the world as the second largest cause of death and debility.

Health is not mere absence of disease but a state of physical, mental, social, spiritual and environmental well being. The western science basically deals with the physical health. Mental health is dealt by a psychiatrist and not by a common general practitioner. Spiritual health finds no place at all in spite of widespread spiritual rituals and beliefs. The eastern science on the other hand deals much more comprehensively and covers all aspects of health as defined but unfortunately lacks technologies and advancement especially in the field of emergency care.

According to the concept, mind and body are spiritually one. Each and every disease for practical purposes can be traced to an emotional imbalance. Research has shown that emotions like fear and anxiety are associated with high blood pressure; anger and jealousy with heart attack and paralysis; and greed and possessiveness with obesity, diabetes and heart failures.

According to the Upanishads, the classical eastern philosophical teaching, "You are what your deep rooted desires are". We are infinite choice makers and by changing our perception and our choices, we can change our reality and hence ultimately our body and our health. Instead of worrying about the past or having anxieties of the future, we should learn to live in the present. The body is not a fixed structure but a thinking organism. Each and every of the three trillion cells in the body are thinking cells. However, most of them are concentrated in the heart, stomach, kidney, colon and bronchial tubes. According to the eastern philosophy, the mind is not confined to the brain but is present in each cell of the body. Many of these cells are even more reliable thinkers than the brain.

Disease occurs when we do not live according to our inner intelligence known as the Dharma. The responsibility for the illnesses and cures resides within us. Living with the law of nature and understanding these laws can help in preventing most of the diseases.

Today the western approach is geared for advances in the treatment of acute illnesses which of course is life saving but when it comes to chronic illnesses the western approach does not have much to offer. The western model has been framed on the concept of understanding the mechanism of disease while the eastern model is based on the philosophy of understanding the origin of the disease.

The mechanism of the disease deals with identifying the organisms or an outside influence. Understanding the origin of disease deals with eating, breathing, digestion, metabolism, eliminating thoughts, feelings, emotions, desires, memories, sleep and relational aspects of a human being. By concentrating on the genesis of a disease one can influence 90 percent of the outcome of a chronic disease.

Ayurveda, prominent name in the eastern system, is a science with a difference. The word Ayurveda is the combination of two Sanskrit words meaning life and knowledge. The 6000 year old holistic system of healing and prolonging life considers all aspects of a person's existence from life and environment through mind and consciousness.

While dealing with addiction the western model for example will ask the patient to quit smoking. On the other hand, the eastern approach deals with the origin of addiction at the mind level itself and motivates the circumstances by which the person himself will give up the addiction.

Heart attack, paralysis, high blood pressure, diabetes, insomnia, cancer, acid peptic disease, infertility, dysmenorrhea etc. now are classified into lifestyle disorders. To a large extent these can be controlled and prevented by changing the lifestyle the body-mind way. The lifestyle disease is nothing but the manifestations of the mind. By improving the power of interpretation and analysis, and by cultivating good thoughts one can change the present situation and alter the occurrence of a disease. By combining the eastern philosophy with the western technologies and advancement one can prevent the disease, control the ongoing biological process, regress the damage done, curtail the dose of various medicines and even avoid using these medicines in future.

Meditation is, in fact, a very good way of balancing oneself against the onslaught of stress. It has been proved beyond doubt that meditation in any form is very good for the body. The inward journey from the disturbed state of consciousness to the undisturbed state of consciousness. When this is attained with the help of primordial sound, it is called Primordial Sound Meditation (PSM).

Meditation is not acquiring Samadhi or a thoughtless state of mind but is the process of attaining that state of mind. The silent spaces in between the thoughts are sources of a pure potentiality with infinite possibilities. Inserting intents in that state of mind (sutra of advance meditation) increases.

According to the eastern philosophy, the body can be defined as made up of three components. The physical body consisting of food and pranic layer, subtle layer consisting of mind, intellect and ego and lastly the casual body consisting of soul, consciousness or the spirit. The soul can be equated to the undisturbed state of consciousness and subtle layer to the disturbed state. It is like an ocean where superficial layers represent the subtle body and the calm and still bottom the consciousness. Yoga is nothing but the union of physical body with the casual body which can only be achieved by controlling the subtle body.

The first basic principle of yogic meditation involves acquiring efficiency in any action performed and be consciously aware of the present. The conscious awareness leads one away from the miseries of the past and anxieties of the future. To give one example while eating breakfast one should concentrate on the meal and not think about something else. Practising conscious awareness of each and every action is the first step in acquiring spiritual health. Breathing awareness, eating awareness, thinking awareness etc. all are the practical ways of doing the same thing. The second step in Yoga is to balance yourself between loss and gain and to maintain tranquillity of mind at all times, places and situations. Every opportunity good or bad should be taken as an opportunity to learn for the future betterment. Various mental exercises are taught to acquire this state of mind. Let go of the attachment, to the results of an action is what the third step propagates for acquiring internal yoga.

Repression and suppression of the thoughts are the fundamental causes of diseases. Fear, doubts and attachment are the three basic fundamental root causes for the development of diseases.

According to the *Bhagwad Gita,* five gateways to hell or acquiring a disease are **attachment, anger, greed, desire and ego.** Many scientists considered doubts, expectations and denial to be the root cause of a disease. Persistence of negativity in the mind is what is responsible for most of the disorders.

According to *Yogasutras* of Patanjali, to remove the negative thoughts of mind, opposite thoughts should be cultivated. The eastern philosophy basically teaches the ways to acquire and cultivate these opposite thoughts of love, compassion and happiness.

The Weather and Health

The weather undoubtedly has the power to affect our moods and health, both psychologically and physically. Psychologists have long proved that our mood is affected by dark clouds and rain, that long dreary winters when the sun is not seen causes depression and that bright sunlight causes mood elevation.

While one has to guard against waterborne diseases and flies during the monsoons as these cause stomach ailments, one has to be careful to protect oneself against chills, draughts and colds during winter. Adequate warm clothing is an essential feature of this season.

However, since ours is a predominantly hot country in which some parts do not even experience winter, given below are a few tips to cope with the summer heat.

With atmospheric temperatures rising, the number of deaths attributed to excessive heat exposure goes up. But most tragedies can be avoided by taking a few precautions, according to physiologists.

1. While the human body tends to adjust to the heat, sometimes, the sudden rise in temperature doesn't allow enough time for the body to adapt to it. When the body is unable to cope with excessive heat, the result is heat exhaustion or heat stroke.
2. Under normal circumstances, humans need about two weeks to acclimatize to a dramatic change in temperature.
3. Symptoms of heat exhaustion include fatigue, nausea, cramps, headache, dizziness and uncoordinated movement. People with heat exhaustion should stop working or exercising; move into shade or air conditioning or take a cool shower; drink fluids to replace lost salt; and rest. If left untreated, heat exhaustion can progress to heat stroke, a more serious condition that can be fatal.
4. With heat stroke, the body simply shuts down the mechanisms for cooling. It stops sweating, so the skin becomes dry; the blood vessels close to the skin constrict, not allowing blood flow to the skin, so there's less cooling.

The temperature rises to over 104 degrees, which can cause brain damage that interferes with breathing and circulation. Common symptoms of heat stroke include dizziness, confusion, unconsciousness, rapid and strong pulse, and hot, dry skin. Children, older people, and those engaged in heavy physical labour are most vulnerable to heat exhaustion or heat stroke.

5. The elderly do not feel as thirsty as younger people do with the same amount of fluid loss, so they are more vulnerable to becoming dehydrated. People on diuretics or tranquillizers are more susceptible to heat exhaustion, as are those with high blood pressure, diabetes or an overactive thyroid.

For people dealing with hot weather, physiologists offer the following tips:

Drink plenty of fluids, but avoid alcohol and caffeinated drinks because they promote dehydration.

Find shade or air conditioning if possible. Even two hours of air conditioning each day can significantly reduce the risk of heat-related illness.

Use common sense.

Avoid strenuous jobs and exercising in the heat.

Do not leave children, pets or anyone who has difficulty caring for themselves in a car without ventilation.

Ask children to rest after 30 minutes of outdoor play.

Check periodically on elders and others who live alone.

Consult a pharmacist about medications because some can inhibit sweat or aggravate heat-related conditions.

Food, Dieting, Anorexia and Bulimia

The Bhagvad Gita says that "a man is what he chooses to eat".

All foods are characterised by four basic sets of distinct features. There are three Guna's (nature) present in food- *Sattvik*, *Rajasik* and *Tamasik*. Food has two qualities, hot and cold. The three *Doshas* or humours namely, *Pitta* (bile), *Vayu* (air) and *Kapha* (phlegm). The six *rasas* (tastes)- sweet, sour, pungent, astringent, bitter and salt.

In a traditional home, pungent foods are recommended in summer, sour during the rains, salty in the autumn, sweet for winters, bitter during the frost and astringent in the spring. These combinations had medicinal considerations in order to maintain equilibrium between bile, phlegm and air. Food and pleasure, food and the seasons, food as a metaphor for seduction has long been written about in literature and in the epics. In fact, food is the raison d'etre of our lives, the reason why we live and work so hard. Yet today it appears that every mouthful that we ingest is adding to our weight, causing us ill health and more importantly, a great deal of guilt. As gay fashion designers stride across the fashion world decreeing what should be worn and what should not, they have taken their revenge on the world by deciding that women should forsake their curves and be presented as flat-chested, with no derrieres and decidedly underweight. As teenagers strive to reach the proportions of the models on the ramp, they cannot live up to either Kate Moss or Twiggy and are falling into depression and eating disorders, chief of which are anorexia nervosa and bulimia.

Anorexia, which is also striking Indian teenagers in the big cities as they fit themselves into the tightest of jeans, is a state in which the teenager feels that she will gain love, attention and success only if she is slim. She, therefore, starves herself and insists that she is fat even when she is reduced to skin and bone.

Dieting loses its magnetic draw when you accept and appreciate your physical body as it is instead of focusing on improving it.

The key is to focus not on the calorie burning effects of exercise but on the enjoyment and sheer pleasure of being active. Celebrating your body through physical movement whether it's a four mile run, a gentle stretching session or a hike in the park enhances self-esteem and promotes self acceptance.

Eat sensibly, eat with a relaxed mind and don't feel guilty. Eat junk food too once in a while if it makes you happy.

Exercise and Good Health

Modern conveniences make it essential for us to go to the gym, take a walk, do yoga or any other form of aerobic exercise. Working in an office, sitting in front of computer screens or even house work does not give the body enough exercise to keep fit and trim. The easy availability of exotic, mouth-watering foods in our fridges or at the supermarket will be our undoing if we do not consciously balance our intake with the outflow.

Regular exercise brings sound health to people of all ages. Pick up any book or health magazine and you will find pages about the other benefits of exercise. Undoubtedly, exercise can work wonders.

You will sleep better, wake up fresh, feel more alert, walk erect and look very much younger than your age. Those who have been exercising regularly can appreciate the difference. There are many others who wish to start exercises but do not find the right occasion.

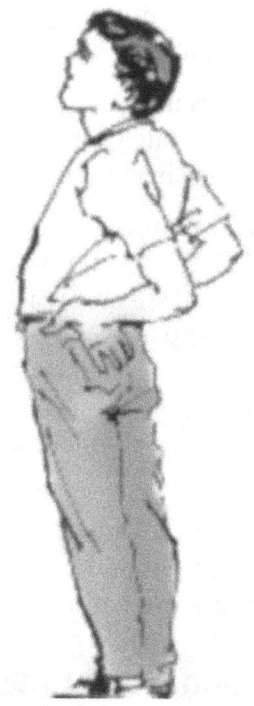

In the first place, people hesitate to start exercising. Once they start, they tend to overdo it so as to get quick results. Some take up strenuous exercises in the beginning itself. This group of people often land in trouble.

Are there many points to be remembered before taking up any strenuous exercise? Should one consult a doctor? The answer is yes. Here are some of the situations where you need to take a doctor's opinion:

1. If you are over 60 years of age and have been doing mild exercises like walking and suddenly plan to take up strenuous activity like tennis, cycling and swimming.

   After a certain age there are many degenerative changes occurring in the body. When the body is put under stress, bones and joints may get stretched causing injury. Besides, the blood supply to heart and brain is compromised and this may have grave consequences.

2. If you are over 40 and have never done any exercise throughout your adulthood.

   After 40 years, several diseases go on for years together without any obvious symptoms or signs. Once the body is put under stress these become manifest, e.g. coronary artery disease.

3. If you are a heavy smoker; smoking more than 20 cigarettes a day.

   Smoking makes blood vessels hard and narrow and therefore the circulation to vital organs may be reduced. While taking up any stressful exercises all of a sudden, some organs may fall short of blood supply. It is always better to build up the level of exercise gradually.

4. If you are overweight, take a doctor's opinion before starting any exercise programme. Obese individuals are a storehouse of many diseases. It is better to undergo a thorough check-up before any exertion to avoid sudden shocks.

5. If you have been suffering from high blood pressure, heart disease or kidney disorders.

6. If you are pregnant, you should not undertake any strenuous exercise as it enhances the chances of abortion in the early stages of pregnancy. However, regular walking should be encouraged as it enhances the sense of well-being and relieves aches and pains associated with pregnancy.

Walking your way to good health

After injuries suffered during jogging and the undue strains of doing aerobic exercises, doctors are increasingly supporting walking as the panacea for many ills. It can be undertaken safely by all age groups and the end results are highly beneficial.

For those who ignore walking as mundane, this is the time to break the myth and discover its benefits. It is an easy path to recovery and also a prescription to healing at times. Walking is a miracle treatment that can alleviate heart diseases, diabetes, arthritis, obesity and depression- a simple remedy of putting one foot in front of the other.

As life becomes hectic by each passing day, some simple activities can help sustain daily pressures. Not many people realise that if in a day, we sit or lie down for more than 15 hours, it is harmful for our posture. Here is a list of a few diseases that can be warded off with just a walk.

Walk away from heart diseases

Heart specialists prescribe walking to heart patients as it may help prevent cardiovascular diseases and in making the heart muscles stronger. Walking also oxygenates every part of the body. The blood-fat level changes to a healthier balance; the levels of artery-clogging blood fats decrease with walking.

One may have to reduce the intensity of an exercise but with an increase in duration and frequency, walking works well as jogging does for the body. "Every step you take, is a step towards a stronger heart and a longer life". Walking also helps prevent a second heart attack in people but they should get the doctor's permission.

Walk away from diabetes

Walking is also strongly recommended to diabetics. It increases the energy level and enhances the ability of the muscles to rake up blood sugar, as a result of that, the requirements for insulin in most people decreases. Walking after a meal is beneficial for most diabetic patients.

Walk away from arthritis

Most people with arthritis may benefit from a regular exercise programme. Walking may be the best exercise for arthritis patients as it helps to strengthen muscles around the joints. This may prevent joint injury and disfigurement and also relieve some of the pain that occurs when bones rub against bones.

The natural tranquillising effects of walking also help to ease arthritic pain. Its mood elevating effect offers an added benefit. Walking can greatly improve a person's attitude but one should not overdo it. One should start walking three or four times a week, and increase the distance by no more than 10 per cent every 2 weeks.

Walk away from obesity

Obesity is always a problem and can lead to other ailments. It is always good to maintain the body weight throughout one's life and

walking is one of the best ways to do it. It shoots up your metabolic rate and you burn more calories.

Walking helps the burning of body fat, building muscle tissues at the same time. As a result, you look much better at a given weight.

Also it increases the muscle mass, has higher metabolic rate than fat, which means that it continuously burns more calories.

Walk away from back pain

Walking can help relieve back-pain by strengthening and toning muscles that make the spine more stable.

Though the general view is that a person should rest when he has back-pain, if a person walks slowly and does not put any strain on his back while walking, it is an effective remedy.

Health Check-Ups

Earlier it used to be said that one should go for a health check-up after the age of 40. But, with the changes in our lifestyle body resistance is lowered these days. Health check-ups can be undertaken from the age of 35.

The frequency of check-ups can be planned as follows:

Up to 35 years - every 3 years

36 to 40 years-every 2 years

After 40 years- Yearly

Most hospitals in big cities have health check-up schemes.

Requirement of an annual health check up?

IMPORTANCE

To know your health status.

To have base line information about your biochemistry.

To know about any systemic problem.

Early detection of any incipient disease.

Primary and secondary preventive measures to be adopted.

Lifestyle intervention strategies to be adopted.

Helps early diagnosis and early treatment and may cure the disease.

Prevents complications.

Improves prognosis.

Determines the frequency of subsequent follow up.

Annual health check up after the age of 20 is a must to keep you healthy and fit.

Sustain health and fitness.

Clinical examinations

Pulse: Normal pulse is 60-80 per minute.

Tachycardia: If pulse is faster (more than 90 per minute)

Bradycardia: If pulse is slow (less than 60 per minute)

Irregular: If there are missed beats or irregular rhythms.

This can be prevented by appropriate life style interventions and necessary medical treatment if detected well in time.

BLOOD PRESSURE

Normal systolic (upper) blood pressure is 110-140 mmHg.

Normal diastolic (lower) blood pressure is 70- 90 mmHg.

HYPERTENSION

Mild when diastolic blood pressure is 90-99mmHg.

Moderate when diastolic to 100-109 mmHg.

Severe when the diastolic blood pressure is more than 110 mmHg.

Systolic Hypertension - when the systolic blood pressure is more than 160 mmHg.

Hypertension is a silent killer. 15-80% of the population after the age of 20 is hypertensive. It is usually detected on routine check up or otherwise. It has been estimated that 60% patients are unaware that they have hypertension, since it does not produce any symptoms in the early stages. Various predisposing factors responsible for hypertension are stress, consumption of excess of salt, consumption of excess of alcohol, fat rich diet, smoking, obesity, lack of exercise, environmental pollution, family history of hypertension, consumption of oral contraceptive pills in women and some of the pharmaceutical preparations containing ephedrine or adrenaline.

Lifestyle intervention such as regular exercise, meditation twice a day, abstinence from smoking, alcohol, ideal body weight, consumption of fresh vegetables and fruits and avoidance of saturated fat can control hypertension to a very large extent.

Every individual should know his/her base line blood pressure after the age of 20. If normal, they should get it checked on a periodical basis once in a year. If hypertensive with or without risk factors then blood pressure may checked, monitored and treated on an individual basis by the treating doctor.

HEART

Heart is evaluated to detect first, second, third or fourth heart sounds or presence of any abnormal murmur, thereby suggesting narrowing or leaking of the valves or presence of any hole in the heart. It is also evaluated for presence of any pericardial rub.

LUNGS

Lungs are evaluated for normal vesicular breathing and for the presence of any abnormal adventitious sounds such as rhonchi (sound produced by narrowing of breathing, tubes bronchioles) usually heard in bronchitis or for presence of any crepitations heard in lung congestion or infection such as pneumonia, tuberculosis or bronchitis. Lungs are also evaluated to find out any evidence of fluid in the pleural cavity (pleural effusion) commonly due to tuberculosis.

LIVER

Liver is evaluated for any enlargement such as fatty liver, hepatitis, alcoholic liver disease and various other disorders. Liver span may reduce in shrunken liver.

SPLEEN

Normally spleen is not palpable. If enlarged it suggests disease process.

KIDNEY

Kidneys are normally not palpable. If enlarged suggests disease process such as infection or malignancy.

INTESTINAL SOUNDS

Normal and abnormal intestinal sounds can be evaluated. Abnormal intestinal sounds may predict intestinal obstruction.

PERIPHERAL VESSELS

Peripheral vessels are evaluated for normal circulation in the periphery. This is of tremendous clinical help in evaluation of blood flow in smokers, diabetics and individuals with narrow peripheral arteries.

PERIPHERAL NERVES

Are evaluated clinically for presence of any motor/sensory neuropathy, especially in diabetics etc.

BONES AND JOINTS

To find out any deformity, arthritis etc.

EYE, ENT AND DENTAL CHECK UP

To evaluate any disease process in eyes, throat, ears, nose and oral cavity.

Investigations

HAEMOGLOBIN

Usually by a drop of blood to find out anaemia (normal haemoglobin is 13-14 gm% in men and 11-13 gm% in women)

TOTAL LEUKOCYTE COUNT (TLC)

This can also be tested by a drop of blood. If the white count is increased we call it as leukocytosis which may suggest infections or malignancy. If the count is very low we call it is leukopenia which suggests compromised white cell count due to various disease processes (normal white cell count is 4000-11,000 per cubic mm).

RED BLOOD CELL COUNT

This reduced in anaemia and the shape of red cells may be microcytic or normocytic. If the red blood cell count is increased we call it as polycyathemia suggesting a disease process. Differential count (DLC) may decrease or increase depending on type of infection or malignancy.

ESR

Erythocyte Sedimentation Rate suggests the time taken by red blood cells to settle down. It may increase in chronic infection, malignancy or anaemia and may reduce when the red blood cell count is high.

BLOOD SUGAR TEST

Normal fasting blood sugar should be 60-100 mg% and post prandial (2 hours after meals) is usually up to 140 mg%. If the reading is above these values an individual is labelled as a diabetic. It also helps us in regular follow up of diabetic patients who are on oral antidiabetic drugs or Insulin.

LIPID PROFILE (CHOLESTEROL)

Normal blood cholesterol is 150-250 mg%. If the cholesterol is more than 250 mg%, then one has higher risk for heart attacks/ strokes. If the cholesterol is low or below normal it increases proneness to malignancy and depression.

Good cholesterol (HDL-High Density Lipoprotein) are protective for heart. Normal HDL is 40-50 mg% in men and 50-69 mg% in women. If HDL is 35% it is a risk factor for heart attacks/ strokes.

BAD CHOLESTEROL (LDL-LOW DENSITY LIPOPROTEIN)

Normally levels are up to 160 mg%. High levels of LDL is a risk factor for premature heart attacks/ strokes.

Triglycerides: normal level of triglycerides are 200 mg%, levels between 200-400 mg% is border line high risk, levels between 400-1000 mg% is high risk and levels above 1000 mg% are very high risk for heart attacks.

Cholesterol fitness can be achieved by regular exercise for 30 minutes daily, abstinence from smoking, alcohol in moderation, (not more than 1 or 2 ounce per day), meditation for 20 minutes twice a day, having diet less in saturated fat with cooking oil having more of poly unsaturated fatty acids and mono unsaturated fatty acids, having optimum body weight, avoiding pot belly obesity and caution for the use of oral contraceptive pills, may increase HDL and reduce LDL, TG.

Have periodical check ups of cholesterol profile as recommended by the doctor.

LIVER FUNCTION TEST

Include serum Bilirubin, SGOT, SGPT and alkaline phosphate to find out any abnormality in the liver function.

BLOOD UREA AND CREATININE

To evaluate kidney functions.

URINE EXAMINATION

To find out presence of protein, sugar, casts, crystals, white blood calls and red blood cells.

X-RAY CHEST

To evaluate any evidence of fluid in the pleural cavity or lung parenchymal disease such as tuberculosis or pneumonitis or malignancy and assessment of heart size.

ELECTROCARDIOGRAM (ECG)

To find out any abnormality in the rate, rhythm and electrical activity of the heart, assess ischaemia, infarction and heart blocks etc.

TREADMILL (STRESS TESTING)

Is a method of making you walk on a machine with graded exercise to evaluate the effort tolerance and assess the reserve of coronary arteries. If the test is positive it suggests a lack of circulation to the heart muscle (ischaemia) thus giving information about the line of treatment. Left ventricular angiography evaluates the status of coronary arteries, LV function and valves. It helps in further management such as CABG, angiography, stenting, valve repair or valve replacement.

COLOUR DOPPLER ECHOCARDIOGRAPHY

Usually required to evaluate heart functions including the status of hole in the heart and other abnormalities.

PULMONARY FUNCTION TEST

To evaluate functional capacity of lungs.

PAPSMEAR

For early cancer detection in women.

Hence, to remain fit and healthy, one has to get annual check ups periodically.

Good Health and Water

Water is an essential component of life. Every cell in our body depends upon water to function properly. Without it we would die in days. Most of us don't understand the role of this vital nutrient. The human body consists mostly of water. Blood is 83% water; muscles 75%; bones 22%. In fact 55-65 % of a woman's body and 65-75% of man's body is made up of water (men generally have more water retaining tissue than women). The average adult body holds 35-50 litres of water, 2.3 to 2.8 litres of which are lost every day through excretion and perspiration.

Some seemingly solid foods are mostly water. Fruits and vegetables are more than three-fourths water. Green beans, for example, are 89% water and lettuce is 95% water. Both of these are actually wetter than milk, which is 87% water. Even meat is about half water and bread about one-third water by weight.

Though thirst is your body's way of signalling you to consume more water, it is an imperfect signal that may turn off before you've drunk enough to satisfy your body needs. Water helps you digest and absorb all nutrients and get rid of both liquid and solid wastes. In fact, inadequate liquid intake may be one factor in chronic constipation.

Water, as an essential component of blood, transports oxygen as well as infection-fighting to where they are needed in your body. It lubricates joints, keeps internal organs from sticking together and skin from shrivelling and drying out. Salts dissolved in water, maintain the proper electrolyte balance inside and outside cells. Water is also part of the body's air conditioning system - the water lost through your skin helps to cool your body. During pregnancy, it provides a protective cushion for the foetus.

To maintain the proper amount of water in your body, you should consume at least six to eight glasses of clear liquids each day and more if you are physically active or sweat a lot. Most people don't consume nearly enough water, particularly in the warmer months when large amounts of body water are lost through perspiration. Pregnant women need extra fluids, and women who are nursing should drink extra liquids daily to help maintain their milk supply. Infants also need more water than adults realize, and in warm weather babies should be offered water in between feedings.

Water comes from many sources - from other liquids such as coffee, tea, milk, beer and soft drinks; from the content of many solid foods; from the body's own metabolic processes. However, the caffeine in coffee, tea and some soft drinks has a diuretic effect that ultimately causes your body to lose (through urination) more water than you consume. Alcohol too tends to dehydrate, which is why you may wake up thirsty after a night of drinking.

Many people confuse "water weight" with fat. The weight you gain after a big meal is usually almost entirely water that you will lose in a few days.

When you go on a diet that produces rapid weight loss - especially one that is high in protein, low in sugars and starches - most of your initial weight loss will be water, not fat. As soon as you slip back into your usual eating habits, you will "gain" back about a kilo of water (not fat, which all you should be losing and all you should be worrying about). While you are losing weight, its important to drink plenty of water to help your kidneys eliminate the toxic wastes produced by the breakdown of body fat.

Diuretics, commonly prescribed to treat high blood pressure and congestive heart failure, are sometimes recommended for women who gain more than 1.5 kilos just before their menstrual periods. However, diuretics should never be taken without a doctor's approval, because in addition to ridding the body of water, they wash out needed salts, sometimes resulting in potassium deficiency. Never use diuretics to try to lose a few kilos quickly. You will lose water, not fat, and that loss is temporary, and you may seriously dehydrate your body.

Some people believe that drinking liquids with meals dilutes digestive enzymes, preventing the body from digesting and absorbing some of the food eaten. It's not true. Water does not rush undigested foods through our digestive tract. In fact, it facilitates digestion, since enzymes work best in a fluid environment. Drinking water or other low calorie liquids before or with your meals can also help you control your weight by creating a sensation of fullness.

Inadequate or inappropriate liquid intake is a common problem among active people, and it contributes to muscle fatigue and poor performance. In extremely hot weather, or during strenuous exercises such as running a marathon, insufficient water intake may actually be life-threatening.

Water is by far the best liquid to drink before, during and after any activity. If after strenuous exercise you need to drink more than three litres of water to replace lost fluid, add a little salt to any additional water you consume. Salt tablets, however, can be extremely dangerous and should not be taken unless they are administered by a doctor for symptoms of salt depletion.

Very sweet drinks draw water into the intestinal tracts (at the expense of our muscles) and may result in cramps during exercise.

On an average, one requires 10-12 glasses (1glass= 200ml) of liquids every day. Hence you need 1.5-2 litres of liquids daily.

Constipation

The Indian systems of medicine, be it ayurveda, naturopathy, or homoeopathy lay a great deal of emphasis on proper elimination. Good health and happiness are closely connected and naturopathy emphasizes that "constipation is the mother of all diseases." Good health encompasses not only proper digestion but its assimilation and the excretion of waste. While the body has two channels by which air and food enter, namely the wind pipe for air and the food pipe for food, there are four outlets for the excretion of waste materials - the lungs, the kidneys, skin and bowels. It is therefore that Mother Nature has designed the body is such a way that outgo should be more than the intake.

Lifestyle diseases such as diabetes, acidity and even asthma and blood pressure can be traced back to improper diet and excretion. Constipation can also aggravate some diseases such as hernia, piles and fissures. So constipation must not be ignored. Today, the problem has even gone down to little children who literally have "no time" to go to the loo as they are yanked out of bed at around 6 a.m. or so and dragged off to catch their school buses. Added to this is the regular intake of processed and refined "junk" foods that are good to taste but which do nothing for one's health.

Some common causes of constipation

Low fibre diet.

Drinking less than 8-10 glasses of water daily.

Emotional stress and anxiety.

Frequently ignoring the call of nature.

Lack of exercise.

Pregnancy.

Regular intake of medicines like pain-killers and antacids.

Frequent travel.

Certain chronic diseases.

Cures

Taking laxatives is not a permanent cure of the problem. Rather it should be tackled by having a proper diet with a high fibre content, drinking adequate water and taking exercise.

Ayurveda recommends a wide range of simple and compound medicines. One of the simple medicines is fruit pulp of cassia, which is to be taken with water twice daily. This softens the stools and increases movement of the intestines which helps evacuation of the stools. Triphala Churna, a compound medicine prepared from three plants, is also very effective for chronic constipation.

According to homoeopathy, long-standing constipation can have several major consequences such as lowered resistance to various diseases, discomfort in the stomach due to flatulence, allergies, migraine and diseases of the digestive system. It recommends an increased intake of water and drinking warm fluids such as warm milk, honey or lemon in warm water as important for controlling constipation.

Non-vegetarian food should be avoided and smoking stopped. Homoeopathic medicines for treatment of constipation depend on the combination of the symptoms. Commonly used medicines include Nux Vomica, for constipation associated with fissures.

Nature cure also considers constipation to be root cause of several diseases such as appendicitis, rheumatism, arthritis, high blood pressure and cancer. This is based on the fact that poison is formed from constipated stools. Drinking at least 10-12 glasses of water everyday is considered to be the most important measure to control constipation.

Other options for the treatment of constipation offered by nature cure include mud packs, cold towel packs, cold hip baths, abdominal packs, enema and regular toilet habits.

The easiest way to deal with and avoid constipation, however, is to:

1. Pay attention to one's diet. A high fibre diet that consists of 70 per cent green leafy and other vegetables.
2. Cereals should form almost 30 per cent of every meal. Three tablespons of wheat bran added to the wheat flour helps maintain normal bowel movements. Further a high fibre diet is effective only if every mouthful of food is chewed at least 15 times.
3. All fruits except banana and jackfruit will relieve constipation. Bael, citrus fruits, grapes and prunes are the best when it comes to relieve the constipation.

How Yoga Fights Stress

Stress has been directly linked to a variety of prevalent ailments such as heart disease, memory loss, migraines, peptic ulcers, faulty child development during pregnancy, diabetes and viral infections like common colds, acidity, impotence and skin diseases. It has been labelled the millennium plague.

It is an accepted fact that yoga contributes to health and peace of mind. But not many know just how it works. Ancient yogis said that yoga increases life force, which does not explain much. But modern research is slowly uncovering the mechanics of yoga and explaining it in terms that can be understood. A person's mental and phycial health depends on brain and body chemicals. Regular practice of hatha yoga actually alters brain chemistry. It slows down the action of the sympathetic nervous system. In practical terms, this means your body does not get flooded with stress hormones as quickly, your blood pressure does not rise everytime you have an argument, and your heart does not start pounding for fear of missing the bus. Regular yoga practice also improves the functioning of the parasympathetic system which controls your ability to relax. Even after a period of stress, you are able to relax and normalise quickly. Blood pressure comes down, the heart rate rerturns to normal and breathing becomes slow and deep. Tense muscles send unnecessary stress signals to the brain but once they are gently stretched in yogic postures, the signals are automatically switched off.

Over time, yogic poses also stimulate sluggish glands into operating more efficiently, and chemical balance is restored. That may explain why yoga can bring down stress related diabetes, high blood pressure and heart disease.

Other stress busters apart from yoga are a positive attitude, meditation, pranayama, massage, exercise, music therapy, dancing and writing.

Stress is simply a response to a challenge or threat. It dulls the body's sense of pain and improves thinking and memory. Extra oxygen, fats and glucose are released in the body. However, when activated too often stress turns chronic and burns down the immune system and turns the body into a hot bed of disease.

The human body has not been designed to drag around frustrations, anxieties, overwork and bad thoughts. The ambitious, the hostile and the competitive sort of people are more susceptible to stress related disorders.

Breathing Correctly

Breathing correctly is an important way to combat stress, disease and the ever increasing pollution. Yogic breathing systems or pranayama can be undertaken by all age groups for a healthier lifestyle.

Sleep and Sleeping Disorders

"Sleep is related to man's deeds", says an old proverb. But today with the late night on all night working and partying syndrome, sleep is at a premium. One of the reasons for disturbances in one's sleeping patterns is the computer which has encouraged people to remain awake till the early hours of the morning while they "surf the net". The presence

of electricity no longer makes it necessary for a man to rise and sleep with the sun, but as in everything else by upsetting the body's natural rhthyms man has created his own problems. In many, insomnia has become a disease that must be treated by taking sleeping tablets and tranquillizers, which in turn give rise to their own problems.

Sleeping disorders or insomnia are the result of:

- Anxiety or tension.
- Environment change such as constant travel.
- Emotional arousal.
- Phobia against sleep or fear of insomnia.
- Pain or discomfort.
- Caffeine and alcohol.

While the days of the legendary Kumbhakaran and Sleeping Beauty are behind us, a good nights sleep is essential to function properly as sleep is indeed the wonder drug that causes the body and mind to heal themselves. A good night's sleep has always been considered a panacea for many ills.

Sleep Well-Hazards to Our Health

Most people know when they have had a perfect night's sleep. They rest without a break and wake up renewed, with a sparkle that lasts the day.

Such nights often follow being stretched to the limit physically or mentally, or accomplishing something. Pleasure is important - a convivial evening often precedes good sleep. And the environment matters: to some people, a dreary bedroom takes a toll on relaxation.

So, if you sleep less soundly than you would like, it is time to improve the quality of your rest - and inject more energy into your day.

Golden rules

A good night's sleep is as important to life as exercise and healthy eating. Go to bed and get up at about the same time most days. Then you can enjoy the occasional late night or early morning without suffering ill effects. For weekend late-nighters, "Sunday insomnia" can put a blight on Mondays. One solution is to forgo a late lie-in on Sunday morning so that you are tired by bedtime. Plan pleasurable wind-down activities on Sunday evening.

Avoid heavy, rich meals and foods high in calcium and magnesium, such as nuts.

Bedtime rituals

Try the following:

Along, warm bath with soothing aromatherapy oils, candles and music.

Read a book in the bath.

Try hot milk, which contains tryptophan, a natural tranquilliser, or yoghurt.

Take a five-minute, leisurely walk.

Treat yourself to a night cap, but only if you have not had a drink all day.

Mattress support

Support without sag is the key, says physiotherapist Wendy Emberson.

"When lying on your side, the bony bits - hips, shoulders and knees - should sink in so that the waist and spine are supported. This does not happen with an "orthopaedic mattress', which means your spine and joints are under strain."

When buying a new bed, don't just lie flat on it for 30 seconds, looking embarrassed. Try each bed for five minutes or more, in a variety of sleeping positions. The average weight difference between men and women is 25 kg, so you might prefer two single mattresses that bolt together. Mattresses should be turned regularly. If you have a bad back or arthritis, a good mattress can vastly improve the quality of sleep. You will also feel less stiff in the morning.

Pillow talk

One pillow only is the general rule. One man began to suffer such bad headaches that he feared a brain tumour. He had been sleeping on his front with five pillows; after changing to one, his 'headache" vanished. Nerve compression when the neck is under strain can also lead to the frightening sensation of a "dead" arm.

When lying on your back, a good pillow should fit into the nape of your neck. When sleeping on your side, the pillow should fill the space between your ear and shoulder; scrunch it up if necessary. People with broad shoulders sometimes prefer a high, harder pillow. To avoid neck problems on a holiday, take your pillow with you.

Some people, because of heartburn, breathing problems or snoring, like to sleep propped up. Rather than adding pillows, it is best to raise the head of the bed by placing the legs on a brick. This keeps the neck and spine straight.

The best position

Whether flat on your back, curled up in a foetal position or on your front with arms splayed like a windmill, sleep position is largely a habit. In fact, we change positions is largely a habit. In fact, we change positions about 60 times a night.

Hazards to Our Health from Pollution

Water pollution

Considering a WHO study pointed out almost a decade ago, 80 per cent of the deaths in our country are caused by water-related diseases every time we drink a glass of water".

Our drinking water comes from two sources: surface water and groundwater. After surface water - rivers, lakes and canals - was declared polluted some decades ago, there was a race to switch to 'safer' groundwater. But the bad news is that today surface water is more polluted than ever and groundwater is far from safe. Scientists at the National Environment Engineering and Research Institute have concluded that 70 per cent of the available water in India is polluted.

The three main sources of water pollution are industry, agriculture and municipal users.

"Waste from our households accounts for almost 80 per cent of all pollutants." So in the absence of proper sewage and water treatment facilities, people across the country are consuming their own rubbish and excreta.

Add to this the agricultural waste that trickles into the surface water in and around cities. Nitrates, sulphates and fluorides - poisonous components found in fertilisers and agrochemicals - flow down in large quantities into rivers and canals from fields surrounding them. Excessive accumulation of nitrates give rise to cancerous growths in the human gastroinstestinal tract. Sulphates attack the alimentary canal and fluorides teeth.

Pesticides, handy tools for suicide scenes in Hindi films, get washed down by rain and collect in low lying areas near a river and seep into it. Pesticides and fertilisers manufacturers play a major role in poisoning us. Although the Water Act (1974), makes dumping of effluents into water illegal, a few large and most medium and small scale units indulge in it regardless. Other high-polluting industries - distilleries, tanneries; pulp and paper, electroplating, textiles and dyeing units - pump in heavy metals, phenols, cyanide, oil and grease, which are extremely difficult to treat. Their accumulation in the human body over a long period can be fatal.

Most of them don't bother to install mandatory treatment plants and some which do, don't operate them as the costs are huge.

The main reason for groundwater pollution is the culture of over dependence on it. Industrialisation and the population explosion has dried out the shallow layers and in the absence of regular regeneration, the concentration of pollutants have become abnormally high in the ground-water.

Apart from the pollutants which percolate and seep into the groundwater from the top, its excessive mining has lead to a relatively new problem - widespread poisoning of arsenic, a known carcinogen - in West Bengal and more recently a calamity situation in neighbouring Bangladesh.

At an international conference on arsenic poisoning of groundwater in Dhaka in February, global experts discussed ways to combat what is possibly the largest mass poisoning case in the world with more than 50 million people at risk.

The calamity has occurred due to large-scale withdrawal of groundwater - 97 per cent of Bangladesh uses groundwater - which gradually denuded the arsenic deposited under the fertile Bengal delta which found its way into drinking water by leaching in shallow aquifers causing arsenicosis. The problem has reached such alarming proportions because of late detection of the problem as the toxicity may take 8 to 14 years to manifest itself.

If you now think only bottled mineral water is safe - think again. For, experts claim that many quick buck seekers in every corner of the country are simply drawing out groundwater into bottles, adding a bit of carbon-dioxide to it for sparkle and flooding the market.

Food pollution

The manufacturer doesn't care about what he's putting into your food, and neither does the government

Before you bite into that *jalebi*, think a moment. You know, of course, that it is filled with oil (which will clog your arteries) and sugar (which will interfere with your metabolism). But those aren't the only poisons that *jalebi* contains. The oil has probably been hydrogenated which can cause cancer. Look at the maker of the jalebis. Do you think he cares what colouring agents he puts in? Do you think he's bothered about the possibilities of adding carcinogenic properties?

But then the jalebi-maker is not alone. You might even say you're taking your chances eating his wares from an uncovered stall on that dirty thoroughfare. But what do you do when some of the reputed brand names are also in there, popping a poison or two into their preparations?

Consider this list of horror stories from the mouth of hell:

In 1995, the government banned candy floss, on the grounds that it contained cancer-causing agents that harmed the liver, the spleen, the kidneys and the brain. Candy floss is back. Are the contaminants back too?

The food colouring often used in *sevganthia*, *jalebis* and Mughlai *pulao* is Metanil yellow which has been proved to cause cancer, anaemia, paralysis and even mental retardation in the young. That could, of course, be the result of the turmeric powder used which is often contaminated with Metanil yellow so that the manufacturers can stint on the amount of turmeric they put in.

Or you could find that the red chilli powder you're using has Sudan red in it, another colouring chemical that causes paralysis and cancer.

Deep-fried samosas, stored ketchups, cheese and mushrooms, sausages, salted fish and seafood are rich in nitrosoamines which can give you cancer.

Any baked crunchy is likely to overdose you with salt and give you hypertension and even kidney problems.

So what's safe? Fruit? Not unless its organically grown. If its been sprayed with DDT, you'd better wash it or you'll choke to death. DDT accumulates in the system and prevents the body from absorbing oxygen, which eventually causes asphyxiation. But even washing may not do it because DDT can penetrate the top layers of thin-skinned fruit and dissolve into it. And if you suddenly find an apple or a melon that is sweeter than normal, it might have been injected with a banned carcinogenic sweetener, many of which are cheaper than sugar and have 500 times its sweetening power.

Various bodies have tried to control and moderate the use of these poisons but the problem has always been policing. There are laws, there are penalties but we still haven't cracked the problem of putting them into practice.

Air pollution

The poisonous air in Indian cities has set a new record in WHO reports. And it's killer.

Millions of Delhiites suffering from respiratory disorders, cannot deny that there is something wrong in the composition of air in their metropolis. Instead of the regular 20-79-1 per cent ratio of oxygen, nitrogen and other gases, there are large quantities of oxides, suspended particles and toxic compounds which play havoc with our lungs. The situation is no different in Mumbai, where breathing is equivalent to consuming 10 cigarettes a day. Or in any other Indian city. Spiralling levels of air pollution - that urban curse - have made gas chambers of our business hubs.

"The main culprit as far as air pollution in cities goes is exhaust from vehicles, followed by industries, and lastly, burning of refuse".

Even as new urban centres and mini-Mumbais spring up all over India, a study by a Delhi-based NGO, the Centre for Science and Environment, revealed a shocking figure: there are an estimated 51,779 deaths every year in Indian cities because of air pollution.

Indeed, pollution was never so assisted as in an urban set-up. To beat the heat, you travel in an AC car, but in the process you aid the production of ozone, which can damage the respiratory cilia and cause chest pain.

We might as well rework the standard line taught to Class I students: polluted air is every where. The levels of sulphur dioxide, carbon monoxide, hydrocarbons and suspended particulate matter (SPM) in Indian cities far exceed the limits set by the World Health

Organisation. Consider SPM pollution levels stated by a WHO/UNEP study in 1996. Delhi ranked fourth, while Calcutta was sixth and Mumbai thirteenth. Ahmedabad, Calcutta, Kanpur and Nagpur too find a mention in environmental impact studies.

Ultimately, it is the human body which has to pay the price for man-made pollution. Increased levels of sulphur dioxide, particulate matter and ozone can lead to irritation in the eyes, nose and throat and frequent colds, to serious ailments such as asthma, chronic bronchitis, lung fibrosis and cancer. Taking in carbon monoxide reduces the amount of oxygen reaching the brain, thus causing angina, giddiness and confusion. Lead, which is released from petrol-run vehicles, affects the liver and brain and leads to learning disabilities in children. A World Bank study in 1992 had stated that 40,351 permature deaths in 36 Indian cities were due to ambient air pollution levels exceeding WHO standards.

Dust pollution

All the dust that we inhale does not produce disease because there is an inherent protective mechanism in the lungs and respiratory tract.

Dust may be fibrogenic, irritant, inert and allergic. The ability of dust to produce adverse health effects depends on:

   i. Nature of dust and its physio-chemical properties.
  ii. Concentration of free silica in the dust.
 iii. Duration of exposure.
  iv. Health status including presence/absence of tuberculosis, asthma, bronchitis, etc.
   v. Individual susceptibility such as bronchopulmonary clearing mechanism, genetic disorders and smoking habits.
  vi. Use and efficiency of the protective equipment.

Health Effects

   i. Dust may aggravate already existing respirator illness such as asthma, bronchitis and tuberculosis.
  ii. Respirable particles may get deposited in the lungs and depending on their nature may produce a type of lung disease generally known as Pneumoconiosis, which means presence of dust in the lungs and the tissues, reaction to its presence.
 iii. Among the different types of Pneumoconiosis we are more concerned with silicosis. It is a progressive disease and may be associated with tuberculosis. It may take 20 to 25 years for the individual to develop the disease. There may or may not be symptoms. The symptoms, if present, are dysponea (breathlessness), dry cough, feverish feeling and chest pain.
  iv. Coal dust produces coal workers pneumoconiosis, and aggravates the existing chest diseases.
   v. Inhalation of iron oxide particles or iron dust produces sclerosis which is a mild pneumoconiosis and reversible condition.
  vi. Nuisance dust may also irritate the eyes, the upper respiratory tract and skin.

You can help yourself

a) Ensure proper maintenance of in-built ventilation system. Inform supervisors of any failure of dedusting mechanism.
b) Maintain good housekeeping and ventilation.

c) Do not smoke! Smoking is known to increase respiratory illness.
d) Please bring to the notice of the doctor any chronic respiratory illness such as tuberculosis, bronchial asthma, bronchitis, etc. Use appropriate dust masks and replace filters at periodic intervals.
e) Do not confuse dust masks with gas masks. These cannot be interchanged.

Food and Nutrition

Human nutrition is the study of how food affects the health and survival of the human body. Without food our bodies cannot stay warm, build or repair tissues or maintain a heart beat. Eating the right foods can help us avoid certain diseases. These and other important functions are fuelled by chemical substances in our food called nutrients. These are classified as:

Water helps the absorption of the food materials through the digestive tract. A person can survive only 8-10 days without water. Water also maintains a natural balance between dissolved salts and water inside and outside of cells. While water has no calorific value without it in our diet we cannot digest or absorb the foods we eat or eliminate the body's digestive waste.

Carbohydrates are the human body's key source of energy providing 4 calories of energy per gram. When carbohydrates are broken down by the body, the sugar glucose is produced. Glucose is critical to help maintain tissue protein, metabolise fat, and fuel the central nervous system.

Proteins help build and repair body tissues from hair and fingernails to muscles. In addition to this proteins speed up chemical reactions in the body, serve as chemical messengers, fight infection and transport oxygen from lungs to the body tissue. Although protein produces 4 calories of energy per gram, the body uses proteins for energy only if carbohydrates and fat intake is insufficient. When tapped as an energy source protein is diverted, from the many critical functions it performs for our bodies.

Fats provide 9 calories of energy per gram. They are the most concentrated of the energy producing nutrients, so our bodies need only very small quantities. Fats play an important role in building the membranes that surround our cells and in helping blood to clot. Once digested and absorbed, fats help the body absorb certain vitamins. Fats stored in the body cushion vital organs and protect us from extreme cold and heat.

Vitamins and minerals are needed by the body in very small amount to trigger the chemical reactions necessary to maintain good health.

Storing Food

It is necessary for every housewife to have a fair knowledge of the purchase and storage of food. Given below are a few helpful hints—

Rice, pulses and legumes should be stored in air tight tins.

Flour and *maida* can be stored in air tight polythene bags and kept in the fridge. Alternatively one could use air tight containers. Keep whole grain flours in cool and dry place.

Fruits and vegetables

Keep all vegetables in the fridge in separate polythene bags.

Cut lemons and grapefruit will keep moist if placed cut side down on a saucer.

Wash and trim fresh green vegetables before storing.

Fruits should be ripened at room temperature and then put away in the refrigerator.

Do not cut fruits until ready to use.

To keep asparagus fresh, cut a small amount off the bottom of each stalk. Stand the stalk upright in a container in a small amount of water, cover with a plastic bag and refrigerate.

Before storing root vegetables e.g. carrots cut off their leafy green tops.

Sorting out vegetables before putting them away is a must.

Open bundles of palak, remove rotten leaves and other weeds. Then wrap them in a double sheet of newspaper. Put in a large polythene bag and store in the fridge.

Remove leaves and stalks from cauliflower before putting them away.

Ensure to turn polythene bags inside out or dry them out from time to time as vegetables tend to sweat due to the moisture content in them. This will prevent moisture dripping from the glass cover of the tray and spoiling the vegetables.

Store chillies and ginger in plastic or glass containers inside the fridge.

Dhania can be stored by dipping their roots in a glass of water and standing them at the back of the fridge.

Store lemons in polythene bags.

Keep vegetables and fruits in the fridge because there are certain enzymes in the fruits and vegetables which combine with oxygen from the atmosphere and destroy the vitamins present in them. These enzymes are inactive when food is kept chilled, so fruits and vegetables should be kept in the fridge immediately.

Bananas, oranges and potatoes, are usually never kept in the refrigerator because the reason is simple. These fruits and vegetables have a thick peel which protects the vitamins.

Dairy products

Paneer will keep fresh longer if it is refrigerated upside down in original carton

Before putting away an opened carton of ice-cream in the freezer press plastic wrap on to the surface of the ice-cream.

To check freshness of an egg put in a container of cold water, if it floats to the top its too old to use.

To preserve left over egg whites pour into plastic ice cubes tray and freeze.

Milk and cream should be covered properly. Remove only amount to be used at one time, keep away from foods and flavours.

Use soft cheese quickly. Wrap left over cheese tightly in waxed paper.

Fish meat and poultry

Wrap poultry and meat loosely in wax paper to allow air to circulate around the flesh.

Freeze chicken broth in ice-cubes trays. When frozen store in plastic bags.

Wrap bacon in wax paper. Remove only amount to be used at one time.

Wrap fish tightly or leave in store wrapping, cook as soon as possible.

Freezing food

Clean your refrigerator and freezer at regular intervals to control odour.

Prevent odour from spreading by making all food wrapped and covered.

Before refrigerating any liquid ensure that it is in a tightly sealed container.

To cool food quickly before freezing set hot pans in ice water. Wrap the food and freeze it at once.

Maintain a list of frozen foods. This would enable you to cook the older items first.

Frost-free refrigerators have made the task of keeping the fridge clean much easier. However, if you still have a fridge that is not frost free make sure you defrost it. When the frost is 1/4 inches thick, use a dull plastic scraper. After defrosting dip a cloth in glycerine and wipe the freezer coils with it. This will make your task easier the next time over.

How to Buy Medicines Over the Counter

These medicines are available at chemist shops, supermarkets and other stores and do not require a prescription. Nevertheless certain precautions should be taken before buying medicines.

- Read instructions about the dose
- The drug dose is according to the body weight
- If someone between the age of 12-15 is underweight he should be given the dosage for a 12 years old
- Start with smaller doses in old people

Medicines for colds—many types of medicines are available for curing colds. Asthma patients or peptic ulcer patients should refrain from buying aspirin containing cold cures.

Cough syrup—if you have a dry cough with minimal white sputum, you require a Cough suppressant. If you have a cough with sputum you require expectorants. If you have a dry cough with minimal sputum following an attack of cold you can choose any commercial cough syrup, but in case of yellow sputum, never take an over the counter preparation.

Pain killers—are of two kinds paracetamol and aspirin or sometimes both as a combination. Paracetamol is the safest pain killer. Old people, asthma, peptic ulcer and hyperacidity patients should avoid aspirin.

Menu Making for Daily Meals

Increasingly today, members of the family have to rush in different directions be it school or the workplace. Thus the breakfast becomes a meal that is had on the run. Similarly lunch may be had out of a packed tiffin box or bought from the canteen. We seem to forget that in the process we are completely neglecting our bodies. The housewife thus should ensure that while planning for the day, menu making for the day should be the highest on her priority list. The menu should be so planned as to include all the essential nutrients. Balanced meal at least twice a day is a must. Here are some tips:

Turn menu making into a family project.

Try unfamiliar fruits and vegetables.

Try out new recipes. Exchanging recipes with your neighbours and friends or consulting books goes a long way.

Change your meal pattern e.g. instead of serving rice and dal everyday try out a baked dish.

Notice what your family enjoys at restaurants, try to duplicate those dishes at home.

Vary the shapes and colours of vegetables.

Try to liven up the meal by adding a crunchy vegetable salad or raita.

While serving leftover dishes e.g. chicken curry, don't just repeat it - instead reform it e.g. make it into kathi rolls or dry the gravy and use it as a filling for samosas.

Try and include high fibre foods in the diet especially if catering to elderly people.

While cooking red meat ensure that the fat is trimmed properly.

One can serve fresh fruit for desert.

Instead of butter, season foods with lime juice, vinegar or spices.

Pureed vegetables make excellent sauces for fish, poultry and vegetables.

Menu Making for a Party/ Party Cooking

Plan your menu so as to make it interesting, but do not experiment on your guests.

Select dishes that go together in balanced diet formality etc.

Plan your menu so that serving is easy.

Prepare as many dishes as possible ahead of time. Choose recipes that can be made a day or two in advance.

If you cook in advance remember that dishes to be re-heated should be slightly underdone.

Choose dishes that do not call for last minute attention.

If you hire outside help, hire a caterer in advance and always ask to sample his food.

Be aware of your guests' diet, any needs and preference, e.g. vegetarians may prefer salads, dals or raita.

While planning your menu balance rich foods with light foods.

Avoid serving white or light coloured foods together.

Buy the best meat and other foods, do not stinge.

Select fruits and vegetables that are in season as these taste better.

Health Watch

Under this section we will examine the values of food, colour in food, ways of fighting cancer, and water.

Let us first begin with salads. Yes salads. Most doctors and nutritional experts suggest green leafy vegetables as a cure for almost all diseases. But here's the catch, did you know that salad could also kill you!

Salad vegetables are grown in soil which is prone to faecal contamination by animals and humans. It is prone to infestation of worms. Thus chances of contamination are high. These worms work their way from the intestine to the brain. The larvae burrow through the stomach walls and enter the blood vessels from where they are disseminated to tissues, including the central nervous system. Although they remain harmless in muscles, in the brain or spinal cord these cysts degenerate, their outline becomes irregular, fluid oozes out and the content of the cyst becomes turbid. This can result in swellings in the brain or spinal cord. This causes disorders like fits, motor impairment and even paralysis. Eventually, these cysts degenerate and many of them calcify. If these cysts degenerate completely, the swelling may also disappear, this leads to the disappearance of the symptom as well. However, chances of permanent damage cannot be ruled out.

Despite development of technology the endless micro-organisms cannot be put to an end. The increase in the storage life of chilled foods presents the problem of low temperature bacteria such as listeria. Listeria is a resistant bacterium and is responsible for food poisoning from cooked and chilled chicken products which are heated in the microwave. This bacteria also grow on vegetables, e.g. cabbage, cauliflower. Frozen shrimps are also a source of this bacteria. Listeria may also be present in ice-creams.

Hence, prevention is better than cure. Always take the following precautions:

a) Never munch mooli or gajar without first scraping and washing thoroughly.
b) Wash each cabbage separately. Wash the cabbage again after cutting it.
c) While stir frying vegetables, cook it slightly more to kill the parasites.
d) Ensure that children wash their hands before eating.
e) Ensure that your servants follow hygiene rules.
f) Avoid salads at parties and restaurants.
g) Cook all vegetables and meats at high temperatures to destroy listeria and other pathogens.
h) Always pasteurise milk.
i) Disinfect dish cloths in a sodium hypochloride cloth at regular intervals.
j) Clean and disinfect work surfaces, chopping boards and tap handles in kitchen.
k) Keep your fridge clean and cold (between 0-4 degree celsius).
l) Store cooked meat and raw meat separately. The former should be kept in the bottom shelf of the fridge.
m) Clean and disinfect moist surfaces like sinks, toilets, etc.
n) Pregnant women and senior citizens should avoid all soft cheese and pre-packed ready to eat foods.

■■

CHAPTER-2

First Aid

Before rushing to the doctor, all households should have an emergency medical kit which should be kept in an accessible place. It should contain the following items:

- Oral and rectal thermometers
- Flashlight
- Dosage spoon, eyedropper
- Hot water bottle
- Ice bag
- Blunt end scissors
- Tweezers
- Cotton swabs
- Safety matches
- Adhesive bandages in assorted sizes
- Roll of absorbent cotton
- Painkiller
- 3% hydrogen peroxide solution
- Antacid
- Antibiotic ointment
- Decongestant
- Antivomiting compound
- Burnol
- Balm

Work, Emotions and Mental Health

Five out of ten leading causes of disability worldwide are psychiatric in origin. In embracing a materialistic system with its bagful of unfulfilled aspirations and expectations, people complain of feeling brittle, fragmented and tired of the intolerable mercenary routines of life.

The West and the Japanese as also those in Singapore have influenced the world with their concept of the work ethic. A man was expected to work long hours in the office and be virtually wedded to his work rather than to his wife! This gave rise to a new expression "workaholic" in which men put their personal lives on the backburner in order to work, get ahead and achieve success. One's success at work determined one's self-confidence and self-esteem.

Family relationships, romance, sex, children and even one's health took second place to one's all consuming obsession with work. Even today, there are law firms and investment banks in the U.S. where management recruits earn a million but work from 8 a.m. to 11 p.m. Six days a week! By thirty five they have earned enough to retire. In India too, many corporate executives are wedded to their companies, working long hours, travelling endlessly, chasing "targets". Many die premature deaths as they drink, smoke and suffer stress due to this unnatural lifestyle and unrelenting pressure and competition to achieve and succeed.

Achieving the right balance between the workplace and the home or one's personal life is essential to both the well-being of the individual and the organisation. For too long people have been programmed to regard their company's products and services as more important than themselves and their personal lives. In doing so, one not only loses the correct perspective between work and home but often in losing one's spouse or the children, work suffers. Peter Bolt, an American management consultant today emphasises, that if we live to work, rather than work to live, our lives will be out of balance and we will fail on all fronts!

'Don't worry, be happy' say the lyrics of a hit song and it was popular because most people want to be happy. Happiness, high self-esteem, optimism are all linked together and contribute towards our physical and mental well-being. If you are happy there are more chances that you will be healthy and not suffer the pangs of ulcers or the trauma of insomnia.

Rules for mental health

- Postpone until tomorrow what you are worrying about today.
- Don't brood over the past, plan for the future.
- Make the best of any situation.
- Limit your desires to things which are reasonable and attainable.
- Cultivate a tolerant attitude.
- Develop a sense of humour.
- Find a hobby to occupy yourself. Try and keep busy at all times.
- Share whatever is troubling you with others it will lighten the burden on you

Saving energy

- Plan your work so that you do most of it while sitting.
- Stand straight with your weight borne by the bony framework. This puts minimum strain on muscles and ligaments.
- Stand straight from hips to neck.
- To save your back, bend at the ankles or hips.
- Use whole body at centre if any weight to be removed.
- Take a break after every hour of work.
- Have tables and working surface at the correct height.
- While carrying packages hold the body in balance.
- Use labour saving devices when you can

Caring for the Sick

When somebody is ill in the house the doctor may want a record of the following:

a) Temperature.
b) Quality and duration of sleep.
c) Frequency and quality of bowel movement.
d) Quantity of urine passed in 24 hours.
e) Items and amount of food consumed.
f) Amount of liquids taken.
g) Mood of the patient.
h) Complaints that a patient may have.
i) Ensure that the patient has fresh and clean sheets everyday.
j) Do not allow any wrinkles to be left, smoothen the sheet and tuck tightly on the head and foot of the bed.

- Brush the patient's hair, wash his hands and face. A daily spongie bath is refreshing.
- If the disease is communicable ensure that all eating and drinking utensils

are washed with soap and water. Scald with boiling water after each use by the patient. Keep the patient's utensils separate from the other members of the family. In case of an extremely contagious disease the linen, mattress, and clothing should be burned.

Advice to the person taking care of the patient

- The person should maintain a cheerful and sympathetic attitude.
- Wash your hands with soap immediately after each handling of the patient.
- The attendant should strictly obey all orders of the physician regarding the care of the patient.

Food needs of the patient

Liquid diet—Includes milk or milk drinks, fruit and vegetable juices, soups, coffee, tea or cocoa.

Soft and bland diet includes—any of the above plus pureed vegetables, toast, cereals, custard, eggs, ice-cream.

Light diet—includes any of the above plus baked or steamed fruits or vegetable, chopped chicken.

Diabetic diet—includes minimum sugar and calories and limited protein.

Cardiac diet—minimum salt

Anti constipation diet—Bulky foods, food rich in fibre, whole cereals, fruits, vegetables and fluids.

High calorie diet—large portion of starches and fats.

Low calorie diet—minimum fats, starches, sugar, leafy green vegetables.

Alternative Therapy

Reiki

Reiki is a complete system for activating and putting to use natural energy to promote healing, personal growth, transformation, and enlightenment.

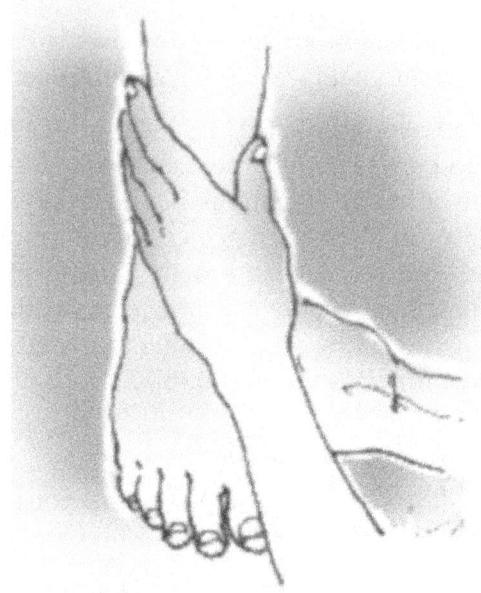

What is Reiki: 'Rei' means 'universal', 'ki' means 'life force'. A method of self-healing founded by a Japanese missionary Mikao Usui. It is not a religion.

Who can learn Reiki: Anyone, including children. It can be taught in any language.

How does Reiki Heal: By flowing through the affected parts of the energy field and charging them with positive energy. The energy flows just by placing your hands. However, some Reiki masters can heal over distances too.

What can be Treated: Almost every illness or injury. It is almost always beneficial and has no side-effects. It works to improve the results of other types of medical treatment, reduing negative side-effects, shortening healing time, reducing or eliminating pain, and lowering stress and creating optimism.

Third degree Reiki: This is also called the maxey degree. At this level the person is ready to learn the intricate process of passing Reiki energy and activate it in others through transmissions called 'attunements'.

One can also take the master teacher level Reiki. This introduces the teacher to another symbol RAKU. It enables the teacher to teach the student now to place the symbols in the field of Reiki.

Urine therapy

Urine Therapy consists of two main parts :

    a) Internal application
    b) External application

The former implies taking urine inside the body and letting the urine come in contact with the mucous membrane. The latter implies rubbing urine on the skin.

If you practise urine therapy you should drink it once or twice a day. The best time to do so is in the morning. If you are suffering from some disease then drink it several times a day including the first urine of the day.

Water therapy

To maintain the proper amount of water in your body consume at least 6-8 glasses of clear liquids each day and more if you are physically active or sweat a lot.

Pregnant women need extra fluids. Infants also need more water than adults. In warm weather babies should be given water between feedings.

Acupressure

It is an ancient and simple oriental therapy which is prevalent even today. Though accupressure is easy and simple it is an effective treatment and can be taken by an individual in the privacy of his own home. This treatment can be taken as often as possible.

Home Remedies

Anaemia

Vitamin B 12: Vitamin B 12 is needed for preventing or curing anaemia. This vitamin is usually found in animal protein, especially in meats such as kidney and liver. There are, however, other equally good sources of Vitamin B 12 such as dairy products which also contain some B 12.

Beetroots: Beetroots are very helpful in curing anaemia. Beet juice contains potassium, phosphorus, calcium, sulphur, iodine, iron, copper, carbohydrates, protein, fat, vitamins B1, B 2, B 6 niacin, and vitamin P. With their high iron content, beets help in the formation of red blood cells. The juice of red beet strengthens the body's powers of resistance and has proved to be an excellent remedy for anaemia, especially for children and teenagers, where other blood-forming remedies have failed.

Fenugreek: The leaves of fenugreek help in many ways. The cooked leaves should be taken by adolescent girls to prevent anaemia, which may occur due to the onset of puberty and menstruation. The seeds of fenugreek are also a valuable cure for anaemia, being rich in iron. The leaves and seeds are useful for diabetic patients.

Lettuce: Lettuce is another effective remedy for this ailment as it contains a considerable amount of iron. It can, therefore, be used as a good tonic food for anaemia. The iron in it is easily absorbed by the body.

Spinach: This leafy vegetable is a valuable source of high grade iron. After its absorption, it helps in the formation of haemoglobin and red blood cells. It is thus beneficial in building up the blood, and in the prevention and treatment of anaemia.

Asthma

Honey: Honey is one of the most common home remedies for asthma. It is said that if a jug of honey is held under the nose of an asthma patient and he inhales the air that comes into contact with it, he starts breathing easier and deeper. The effect lasts for an hour or so. One to two teaspoonfuls of honey provide relief. Honey can also be taken in a cup of milk or water. Honey thins out accumulated mucus and helps its elimination from the respiratory passages. It also tones up the pulmonary lining and thereby prevents the production of mucus in future. Some authorities recommend one-year old honey for asthma and respiratory diseases.

Figs: Among fruits, figs have proved very valuable in asthma. They give comfort to the patient by draining off the phlegm. Three or four dry figs should be cleaned thoroughly with warm water and soaked overnight. They should be taken first thing in the morning, along with the water in which they were soaked. This treatment may be continued for about two months.

Lemon: Lemon is another fruit found beneficial in the treatment of asthma. The juice of one lemon, diluted in a glass of water and taken with meals, will bring good results.

Indian Gooseberry: Indian gooseberry has also proved valuable in asthma. Five grams of gooseberry mixed with one tablespoon of honey forms an effective medicinal tonic for the treatment of this disease. It should be taken every morning. When fresh fruit is not available, dry gooseberry powder can be mixed with honey.

Bitter Gourd Roots: The roots of the bitter gourd plant have been used in folk medicine for asthma since ancient times. A teaspoon of the root paste, mixed with an equal amount of honey or juice of the tulsi leaves, given once every night for a month, acts as an excellent medicine for this disease.

Drumstick Leaves: A soup prepared from drumstick leaves, and taken once daily, has been found beneficial in the treatment of asthma. This soup is prepared by adding a handful of leaves to 180 ml of water and boiling it for five minutes. After being allowed to cool, a little salt, pepper, and lime juice may be added to this soup.

Ginger: A teaspoonful of fresh ginger juice, mixed with a cup of fenugreek decoction and honey to taste, acts as an excellent expectorant in cases of asthma. The decoction of fenugreek can be made by mixing one tablespoonful of fenugreek seeds in a cupful of water. This remedy should be taken once in the morning and once in the evening.

Garlic: Garlic is another effective home remedy for asthma. Ten garlic cloves, boiled in 30 ml of milk, make an excellent medicine for the early stages of asthma. This mixture should be taken once daily by the patient. Steaming ginger tea with two minced garlic cloves in it, can also help to keep the problem under control, and should be taken in the morning and evening.

Bishop's Weed: The herb bishop's weed has been found valuable in asthma. Half a teaspoon of bishop's weed should be mixed in a glass of buttermilk and taken twice daily. It is an effective remedy for relieving difficult expectoration caused by dried-up phlegm. A hot poultice of the seeds should be used for dry fomentation to the chest, twice daily. The patient can also inhale steam twice a day from boiling water mixed with ajwain. It will dilate the bronchial passages.

Safflower: Safflower seeds are beneficial in the treatment of bronchial asthma. Half a teaspoon of powder of the dry seeds, mixed with a tablespoon of honey, can be taken once or twice a day in treating this disease. This acts as an expectorant and reduces the spasms by liquefying the tenacious sputum. An infusion of five grams of flowers mixed with one tablespoon of honey, taken once daily, is also useful in this disease.

Linseed: A decoction of linseed is also considered useful in curing congestion in asthma and preventing recurrence of attacks. The decoction prepared by boiling a teaspoon of linseed powder and a piece of palm candy in two cups of water till the mixture is reduced to half. This decoction taken with a tablespoon of milk once daily, will provide relief from chest congestion. Simultaneously, a linseed poultice should be applied externally during the attack, at the lung bases.

Mustard Oil: During the attack, mustard oil, mixed with a little camphor, should be massaged over the back for the chest. This will loosen up phlegm and ease breathing.

Copper: One of the preventive measures to stop attacks of asthma is to drink water which has been kept overnight in a copper vessel. This water, with traces of copper in it, is believed to change one's constitutional tendency to get respiratory problems.

Backache

Garlic: The most important home remedy for backache is the use of garlic. Two or three cloves should be taken every morning to get results. An oil prepared from garlic and rubbed on the back will give great relief. This oil is prepared by frying ten cloves of garlic in 60 ml of oil in a frying pan. Any of the oils which are used as rubefacients, such as mustard oil, sesame oil, and coconut oil can be used according to one's choice. They should be fried on a slow fire till they are brown. After the oil has cooled, it should be applied vigorously on the back, and allowed to remain there for three hours. The patient may, thereafter, take a warm-water bath. This treatment should be continued for at least fifteen days.

Lemon: Lemon is another useful remedy for backache. The juice of one lemon should be mixed with common salt and taken by the patient twice daily. It will give relief.

Chebulic Myroblan: The use of chebulic myroblan is beneficial in the treatment of backache. A small piece of this fruit should be eaten after meals. This will give quick relief.

Vitamin C: Vitamin C has proved valuable in case of severe backaches. About 2,000 mg of this vitamin should be taken daily.

Bronchitis

Turmeric: One of the most effective home remedies for bronchitis is the use of turmeric powder. Half a teaspoon of this powder should be administered with half a glass of milk, two or three times daily. It acts best when taken on an empty stomach.

Ginger: Another effective remedy for bronchitis is a mixture comprising of half a teaspoon each of the powder of ginger, pepper, and cloves, three times a day. It may be licked with honey or taken as an infusion with tea. The mixture of these three ingredients has also antipyretic qualities and is effective in reducing fever accompanying bronchitis. It also tones up the metabolism of the patient.

Chicken pox

Brown Vinegar: The use of brown vinegar is one of the most important among the several home remedies found beneficial in the treatment of chicken pox. Half a cup of this vinegar should be added to a bath of warm water. This will relieve the irritation of the skin.

Oatmeal: A bath of oatmeal is considered a natural remedy for relieving the itch due to chicken pox. This bath is prepared by cooking two cups of oatmeal in two litres of water for fifteen minutes. This mixture is then put into a cloth bag, preferably cotton, and a string is tied tightly around the top. This bag is allowed to float in a tub of warm water, and swished around until the water becomes turbid. Precaution should be taken to ensure that the bag is not torn. The child with chicken pox can splash and play in the water, making sure that water goes over all the scalds, while the pouch of oatmeal can remain in the tub.

Pea Water: Green pea water is another effective remedy for relieving irritation of the skin. The water in which fresh peas have been cooked can be used for this purpose.

Baking Soda: Baking soda is a popular remedy to control the itching in chicken pox. Some baking soda should be put in a glass of water. The child should be sponged with this water, so that the soda dries on the skin. This will keep the child away by this application.

Honey: The use of honey as an external application has also proved valuable in chicken pox. The skin should be smeared with honey. It will help in the healing of the disease within three days.

Carrot and Coriander: A soup prepared from carrots and coriander has been found beneficial in the treatment of chicken pox. About 100 gm of carrots and 60 gm of fresh coriander should be cut into small pieces and boiled for a while. The residue should be discarded. This soup should be taken once a day-decreases toxicity and reduces the duration of the illness. One lemon should be diluted in a glass of warm water, and a teaspoon of honey should be added to it. This should be taken once or twice daily.

Garlic: Garlic soup is an old remedy to reduce the severity of a cold, and should be taken once daily. The soup can be prepared by boiling three or four cloves of chopped garlic in a cup of water. Garlic contains antiseptic and antispasmodic properties, besides several other medicinal virtues. The oil contained in this vegetable helps to open up the respiratory passages. In soup form, it flushes out all toxins from the system and thus helps bring down fever. Five drops of garlic oil combined with a teaspoon of onion juice, and diluted in a cup of water, should be drunk two to three times a day. This has also been found to be very effective in the treatment of common cold.

Ginger: Ginger is another excellent remedy for colds and coughs. About ten grams of ginger should be cut into small pieces and boiled in a cup of water. It should then be strained and half a teaspoon of sugar added to it. This decoction should be drunk when hot. Ginger tea, prepared by adding a few pieces of ginger into boiled water before adding the tea leaves, is also an effective remedy for colds and for fevers resulting from cold. It may be taken twice daily.

Lady's Fingers: Lady's fingers are highly valuable in treating irritation of the throat and a persistent dry cough. This vegetable is rich in mucilage and acts as a drug to allay irritation, swelling, and pain. About 100 gm of lady's fingers should be cut into pieces, and boiled down in half a litre of water to make a decoction. The steam issuing from this decoction may also be inhaled once or twice a day to relieve throat irritation and a dry cough.

Turmeric: Turmeric is an effective remedy for colds and throat irritations. Half a teaspoon of fresh turmeric powder mixed in 30 ml of warm milk, and taken once or twice daily, is a useful prescription for these conditions. Turmeric powder should be put into a hot ladle, milk should then be poured in it and boiled over a slow fire. This mixture should then be drunk by the patient. In case of a running cold, smoke from the burning turmeric should be inhaled. It will increase the discharge from the nose and provide quick relief.

Tamarind and Pepper: Tamarind-pepper *rasam* is also considered an effective home remedy for a cold in South India. Dilute 50 mg tamarind in 250 ml of water. Boil the diluted tamarind water for a few minutes with a teaspoon of hot ghee and half a teaspoon of black pepper powder. This steaming hot rasam has a flushing effect, and should be taken three tines a day. As one takes it, the nose and eyes water and the nasal blockage is cleared.

Vitamin C: According to Dr. Linus Pauling, a Nobel prize winning scientist, the regular intake of vitamin C-75 mg for adults and 35 mg for children-will prevent the common cold. If, however, a cold has already appeared, large doses of this vitamin will relieve the symptoms and shorten its duration. He estimates that one to two grams (1000 mg to 2000 mg) per day is approximately the optimum amount of this vitamin for this purpose. His advice is to swallow one or two 500 mg tablets of vitamin C at the appearance of the first sign of the cold and continue the treatment by taking one to two 500 mg tablets daily.

Headache

Apple: An apple is valuable in all types of headaches. After removing the upper peel and the inner hard portion of a ripe apple, it should be taken with a little salt every morning on an empty stomach in such cases. This should be continued for about a week.

Henna: The flowers of henna have been found valuable in headaches caused by hot sun. The flowers should be rubbed in vinegar and applied over the forehead. This remedy will soon provide relief.

Cinnamon: Cinnamon is useful in headaches caused by exposure to cold air. A fine paste of this spice should be prepared by mixing it with water and it should be applied over the temples and forehead to obtain relief.

Marjoram: The herb marjoram is beneficial in the treatment of a nervous headache. An infusion of the leaves is taken as tea in the treatment of this disorder.

Rosemary: The herb rosemary has been found valuable in headaches resulting from cold. A handful of this herb should be boiled in a litre of water and put in a mug. The head should be covered with a towel and the steam inhaled for as long as the patient can bear. This should be repeated till the headache is relieved.

Other Measures: Other helpful measures in the treatment of headaches are a cleansing enema with water temperature at 37°C, a cold throat pack, frequent applications of towels wrung out from very hot water to the back of the neck, a cold compress at 4.4°C, to 15.6°C, applied to the head and face, or an alternate spinal compress. Hot fomentation over the abdominal region just before retiring relievs headaches caused by stomach and liver upsets.

Hot foot baths are also beneficial in the treatment of chronic headaches. The patient should keep his legs in a tub or bucket filled with hot water at a tempeature of 40°C to 45°C for fifteen minutes every night before retiring. This treatment should be continued for two or three weeks.

Yogic kriyas like *jalneti* and *kunjal*; *pranayamas* like anuloma viloma, shitali, and sitkari; and asanas such as uttanpadasana, sarvangasana, paschimottanasana, halasana, and shavasana are also beneficial in the treatment of headaches.

High blood cholesterol

Lecithin: Lecithin, also a fatty food substance and the most abundant of the phospholipids, is beneficial in case of increase in cholesterol level. It has the ability to break up cholesterol into small particles which can be easily handled by the system. With sufficient intake of lecithin, cholesterol cannot build up against the walls of the arteries and veins. Lecithin also increases the production of bile acids made from cholesterol, thereby reducing its amount in the blood. Egg yolk, vegetable oils, wholegrain cereals, soyabeans, and unpasturised milk are rich sources of lecithin. The cells of the body are also capable of synthesizing it as needed, if several of the B vitamins are present.

Vitamins: Vitamins B6 choline, and inositol are particularly effective in reducing the level of blood cholesterol. Wheat germ, yeast, or vitamin B extracted from bran contain high quantities of these vitamins. Vitamin E also elevates blood lecithin and reduces cholesterol.

The patient should take liberal quantities of vitamin E rich foods such as sunflower seeds, safflower, soyabean oils, butter, and sprouted seeds and grains.

Sunflower Seeds: Sunflower seeds are valuable in lowering high blood cholesterol. They contain a substantial quantity of linoleic acid which is the fat helpful in reducing cholesterol deposits on the walls of arteries. Substituting sunflower seeds for some of the solid fats like butter and cream will, therefore, lead to great improvement in health.

Menstrual problems

Parsley: Parsley is one of the most effective among the several home remedies in the treatment of menstrual disorders. It increases menstruation and assists in the regularisation of the monthly periods. This action is due to the presence of apiol, which is a constituent of the female sex hormone oestrogen. Cramps, which are a result of menstrual irregularities, are relieved and frequently corrected entirely by the regular use of parsley juice, particularly in conjunction with beet juice; or with beet, carrot, and cucumber juices. The recommended quantity is 75ml of each of the four juices.

Ginger: The use of ginger is another effective home remedy for menstrual disorders, especially in cases of painful menstruation and stoppage of menstrual flow. A piece of fresh ginger should be pounded and boiled in a cup of water for a few minutes. The infusion, sweetened with sugar, should be used thrice daily after meals as a medicine for treating this condition.

Sesame Seeds: Sesame seeds are valuable in menstrual problems. Half a teaspoon of powder of these seeds, taken with hot water twice daily, acts excellently in reducing spasmodic pain during menstruation in young, unmarried anaemic girls. Its regular use, two days prior to the expected periods, cures scanty menstruation. A warm hip bath containing a handful of crushed sesame seeds should be simultaneously taken along with this recipe.

Papaya: The unripe papaya helps the contractions of the muscle fibres of the uterus and is thus beneficial in securing a proper menstrual flow. Papaya is especially helpful when menstruation ceases due to stress or fright in young unmarried girls.

Bengal Gram: A bath prepared by putting an entire Bengal gram plant in hot water is beneficial in painful menstruation. The plant also may be used for a sitting steam bath.

Marigold: The herb Marigold, named after the Virgin Mary, is useful in allaying any pain during menstruation and facilitating menstrual flow. An infusion of the herb should be given in doses of one tablespoon twice daily for the treatment of these disorders.

Banana Flower: The use of banana flower is one of the most effective home remedies in the treatment of menorrhagia or excessive menstruation. One banana flower should be cooked and eaten with one cup of curd. This will increase the quantity of progesterone and reduce bleeding.

Coriander Seeds: Coriander seeds are also beneficial in the treatment of excessive menstruation. Six grams of these seeds should be boiled in half a litre of water. This decoction should be taken off the fire when only half the water remains. Sugar candy should be added to it and the patient should drink it when it is still warm.

Mango Bark: The juice of the fresh mango bark is another valuable remedy for heavy bleeding during menstruation. The juice is given with the addition of white of an egg or some mucilage - a kind of vegetable glue obtained from a plant, and a small quantity of the kernel of a poppy. As an alternative, a mixture of 10ml of a fluid extract of the bark, and 120ml of water may be given in doses of one teaspoon every hour or two.

Ashoka: The bark of the Ashoka tree is an effective remedy for excessive blood loss during the monthly period which occurs due to uterine fibroids and other causes. It should be given in the form of decoction in treating this condition.

About 90gm of the bark should be boiled in 30ml of milk and 360ml of water till the total quantity is reduced to about 90 gm. This quantity should be given in one day, in two or three doses. The treatment should commence from the fourth day of the monthly period and should be continued till the bleeding is checked. A fresh decoction should be made for use each day.

Indian Barbery: The herb Indian barbery is also useful in case of excessive bleeding. It should be given in doses of thirteen to twenty-five grams daily.

Rough Chaff: The herb rough chaff is also valuable in excessive menstruation. An infusion of the herb should be prepared by steeping 15gm of rough chaff in 250ml of water and used for treating this condition.

Hermal: The herb hermal is useful in regulating the menstrual periods. It is especially beneficial in painful and difficult menstruation. Two tablespoons of the seeds should be boiled in half a litre of water, till it is reduced by one - third. This decoction should be given in 15 to 30 ml doses.

Hemp: Hemp can be successfully used when menses do not start at the scheduled time. Five large heads of hemps should be boiled in half a litre of water till the water is reduced to half. It should then be strained and drunk before going to bed for two or three nights. This remedy seldom fails.

First Aid

1. Do first things first quickly, quietly and without fuss or panic.
2. Give artificial respiration if breathing has stopped - every second counts.
3. Stop any bleeding.
4. Guard against or treat for shock by moving the casualty as little as possible and handling him gently.

5. Do not attempt too much - do the minimum that is essential to save life and prevent the condition from worsening.
6. Reassure the casualty and those around and thus help to lessen anxiety.
7. Do not allow people to crowd round as fresh air is essential.
8. Do not remove clothes unnecessarily.
9. Arrange for the removal of the casualty to the care of a Doctor or hospital as soon as possible.

Shock

Shock is a condition of severe depression of the vital functions. It is associated with changes in the circulatory system varying from temporary weakness to complete failure. Its severity varies with the nature and extent of the injury and it is a common cause of death following severe injuries.

Type of shock

There are two types of shock:

1. Nerve Shock.
2. Established Shock.

General signs and symptoms of shock

These may vary from a transient attack of faintness to a state of collapse, and there may be:

1. Giddiness and faintness.
2. Coldness.
3. Nausea.
4. Pallor.
5. Cold clammy skin.
6. A slow pulse at first which tends to become progressively more feeble and rapid.
7. Vomiting.
8. Unconsciousness.

General treatment of shock

1. Reassure the casualty.
2. Lay him on his back with the head low and turned to one side unless there is an injury to the head, abdomen or chest when the head and shoulders should be slightly raised and supported. If he has vomited or if there is interference with breathing, place him in the three-quarter prone position.
3. Loosen clothing about the neck, chest and waist.
4. Wrap him in a blanket or rug.
5. If he complains of thirst he may be given sips of water, tea, coffee or other liquid but not alcohol.
6. Do not apply heat or friction to the limbs. Hot water bottles should not be used.

   Special treatment of established shock: Proceed as already described but bear in mind that in severe cases, transfusion and surgery are matters of grave urgency if life is to be saved. It is therefore unwise to delay transfer to hospital for as long as even five minutes except to deal with failing respiration, to stop severe bleeding, to dress a sucking wound of the chest or to secure a limb badly broken.
7. Do not give anything by mouth (the casualty may require an anaesthetic).
8. Tilt the stretcher so that the level of the head is lower than the rest of the body, except in cases of head, chest or abdominal injury.
9. Remove urgently to hospital.

Asphyxia

When the lungs do not get a sufficient supply of fresh air vital organs and the important nerve centres in the brain which regulate their activity are deprived of oxygen and this causes a dangerous condition called Asphyxia.

Causes of asphyxia

1. Causes affecting the Respiratory Tract
   (a) Fluid in the air passages as in drowning.
   (b) Harmful gases or fumes in the air passages, e.g. coal gas, motor exhaust fumes, after-damp, smoke, sewer gas, ammonia.
   Note: Some gases affect the respiratory centre in addition.
   (c) Foreign bodies in the air passages causing choking, e.g. portions of food, artificial teeth, vomited matter in the case of an unconscious person (owing to failure of the action of the epiglottis), tongue falling back in the case of an unconscious person, blood collecting from a fractured jaw.
   (d) Compression of the windpipe, e.g. hanging, strangulation or throttling.
   (e) Smothering, e.g. overlaying an infant, an unconscious person lying face downwards on a pillow.
   (f) Swelling of the tissues within the throat as a result of burns, scalds, corrosives, stings (wasp or bee), or from some diseases affecting the throat.
2. Causes affecting the Respiratory Mechanism
   (a) Pressure on or crushing of the chest resulting from accidents in mines, quarries, sand pits or demolitions, or from pressure in a crowd.
   (b) Spasm of respiratory muscles in the case of certain poisons, e.g. Strychnine, or diseases, e.g. Tetanus (lockjaw).
   (c) Nervous diseases causing paralysis of the muscles of the chest wall or the diaphragm, e.g. Poliomyelitis.
   (d) Electric shock
3. Causes affecting the Respiratory Centre
   (a) Electric shock.
   (b) Stroke by lightning.
   (c) Poisons such as prussic acid and Morphine.
   (d) Some gases.

Signs and symptoms of asphyxia

Early stages:

1. Dizziness and weakness.
2. Shortness of breath.
3. Rapid pulse.
4. Partial loss of consciousness.
5. Swelling of the veins of the neck.
6. Congestion of the face with blueness of cheeks and lips.

   These signs and symptoms may vary with the degree of asphyxia present.
7. The lips, nose, ears, fingers and toes are bluish-grey.
8. Breathing intermittent or absent.
9. Pulse slow and irregular.
10. Complete loss of consciousness.

General rules for treatment of asphyxia

1. Remove the cause if possible or the casualty from the cause.

2. Ensure that there is a free passage for air. In an unconscious person the tongue may fall back and obstruct the air passages. This possibility should be kept constantly in mind if the casualty is lying on his back.
3. Apply artificial respiration immediately. Artificial respiration must be continued until natural breathing is restored, if necessary for a long time unless a doctor decides that further effort will be of no avail.
4. Utilise any help available to:
   (a) Provide warmth, e.g. blankets.
   (b) Provide shelter from the elements.

Treatment in special cases

Drowning: While artificial respiration is being performed, instruct bystanders to remove wet clothing as far as practicable and wrap the casualty in dry blankets or other dry clothing.

Strangulation: Cut and remove the band constricting the throat.

Choking: To dislodge the obstruction bend the casualty's head and shoulders forward, or in the case of a small child hold him up side down, and thump his back hard between the shoulder two finger right to the back of the casualty's throat.

Swelling of the tissues within the throat: If breathing has not ceased or when it has been restored give ice to suck or, failing ice, cold water to sip. Butter, olive oil or medicinal paraffin may also be given.

Suffocation by smoke: Protect yourself by tying a towel, handkerchief or cloth, preferably wet, over your mouth and nose. Keep low and remove the casualty as quickly as possible.

Suffocation by poisonous gas:

i. Before entering any enclosed space known or suspected to contain poisonous gas of any kind, take a deep breath and hold it.

ii. Ensure a free circulation of air by opening or if necessary by breaking doors and windows.

iii. If the gas is lighter than air, keep low; if heavier, remain in the upright position. Remove the casualty as quickly as possible.

iv. In cases where ventilation is not possible and the character of the gas is known to be deadly a suitable gas-mask must be worn. An additional safety precaution is a lifeline.

Miscellaneous conditions

FOREIGN BODY EMBEDDED IN THE EYE

1. Prevent the casualty from rubbing the eye. In the case of a child it may be necessary to get help to keep him still.
2. Seat the casualty facing the light and stand in front of him. Pull down the lower eyelid.
   (a) If the foreign body is seen and does not appear to be embedded or adherent to the eyeball, remove it with the corner of clean handkerchief, preferably white, twirled up and moistened with clean water.
   (b) If the foreign body is embedded in or adherent to the eyeball, do not attempt to remove it but instruct the casualty to close his eyelids. Apply a soft pad of cotton wool and secure it by a bandage. See that medical aid is obtained.
   (c) If the foreign body has not been found and is suspected to be under the upper eyelid, instruct the patient to blink his eyelid under water.

Alternatively, lift the upper lid forward, push the lower lid beneath it and let go both eyelids. The lashes of the lower lid brush the inner surface of the upper one and may dislodge the foreign body. Should the first attempt be unsuccessful, repeat several times. If the foreign body is not dislodged, see that the casualty obtains medical aid as soon as possible, but when medical aid is not available:

i. Seat the casualty facing the light and stand behind him, steadying his head against your chest.
ii. Place a matchstick on the base of his upper eyelid, press it gently backwards and instruct the casualty to look downwards. Take hold of his upper eyelashes and pull the lid over the matchstick, thereby averting the eyelid.
iii. Remove the foreign body with a corner of a clean handkerchief as described in (a) above.
 (d) When a corrosive acid or alkali is suspected, instruct the casualty to blink his eyelid under water or flush the eye with copious supplies of water. Apply a soft pad of cotton wool over his eye and keep the pad in position by a shade or bandage applied lightly, and see that he obtains medical aid as soon as possible.

Foreign body in the ear channel

If an insect has entered in the ear channel fill the ear with olive or salad oil or insert a few drops of surgical spirit; the insect will float and may be removed.

All other foreign bodies should be left in position and the casualty warned not to interfere with them.

See that medical aid is obtained.

Foreign body in the nose

Instruct the casualty to breathe through the mouth. Do not interfere with the foreign body.

See that medical aid is obtained.

Foreign body in the stomach

Pins and other small objects such as coins or buttons may be accidentally swallowed. Smooth objects need not necessarily cause alarm.

Do not give anything by mouth. See that medical aid is obtained without delay.

Fish bone in the throat

These incidents can cause great discomfort with continued retching, coughing and even vomiting. Usually the casualty's alarm is very much exaggerated and not justified by his actual condition. Do not attempt to remove the fishbone but try to allay panic and seek medical aid.

Emergency resuscitation

BACKGROUND TO MOUTH-TO-MOUTH (OR-NOSE) RESPIRATORY AND EXTERNAL CARDIAC RESUSCITATION

1. If the brain is deprived of oxygen for four minutes irreversible changes take place in it. The aim of respiratory resuscitation is the immediate oxygenation of the blood in order to forestall such changes.

   The urgent need for oxygenated blood is such that the lungs should be inflated, if possible, even before attempting to remove debris from the mouth or air passages.

2. The method of choice in respiratory resuscitation is mouth-to-mouth (or

to-nose). Its main advantage is that it can be for example, in case of drowning while the casualty is still in shallow water, or to an individual who is trapped by a fall of earth and who cannot be immediately released. Other advantages are:

(a) It gives the greatest ventilation of the lungs and oxygenation of the blood.
(b) The degree of inflation of the lungs can be assessed by watching the movement of the chest.
(c) It is less tiring, does not require strength, and can be applied by a child.

Difficulty in employing this method, in cases of injury to the mouth or face and for other reasons, is recognised. Alternative methods of resuscitation.

Respiratory resuscitation

3. The first aider must realise that the vital need is to inflate the lungs even though the air has to be blown past an obstruction in the casualty's throat or windpipe.

Delay of one or two seconds may prove fatal.

If in doubt start mouth-to-mouth (or to-nose) inflation.

In such serious emergencies the first aider's equipment is his hands, his mouth and his lungs. For efficient use they must be co-ordinated by training and practice. The well-trained first aider will be conditioned to take the immediate action of inflating the casualty's lungs while simultaneously positioning his head and lower jaw to open the air passage.

(a) Conscious person in upright position, showing open air passages.

(b) In the unconscious casualty lying on his back, the tongue may fall backwards and block the air passages.
(c) If the neck is extended, the head pressed backwards and the lower jaw pushed upwards, the tongue moves forward thus opening the air passages.

Mouth-to-mouth method

4. Depending upon the position of the casualty, whether lying on the ground, supported in shallow water, or on a bench or table, take up a convenient position such as lying, kneeling or standing and work from the side. With the casualty on his back, hold his head in both hands, one hand pressing the head backwards and the other pushing the lower jaw upwards and forwards Open your mouth wide, take a deep breath and in the case of:

(a) An infant or young child - seal your lips round his mouth and nose, blow gently until you see his chest rise then stop and remove your mouth. Repeat this procedure at the rate of twenty times per minute.
(b) An adult - seal your lips round the casualty's mouth while obstructing his nostrils with your cheek; it may be necessary to pinch the nostrils with the fingers. Blow into his lungs and watch for the chest to rise, then remove your mouth. Inflation should be at the rate of ten per minute.

The first six inflations should be given as quickly as possible.

Method of improving the air passage

5. While continuing mouth-to-mouth inflation of the lungs, in the case of:

(a) An infant or young child- place one hand under his neck and raise gently. With the other hand extend the head backwards.

(b) An adult-grasp the back of the head between the hands with the fingers gripping the angles of the jaw. While extending the head backwards push the jaw forwards and upwards.

Not infrequently it will be found that as soon as the air passage is clear and the lungs have been inflated, the casualty will gasp and start to breathe spontaneously.

Gurgling or noisy breathing indicates the need to clear the throat of fluid or debris.

Mouth-to-nose method

6. Should the casualty be in a state of spasm or convulsion and his mouth cannot be opened, or if he has no teeth, it will be necessary to inflate the lungs by the mouth-to-nose method.

Again work from the side of the casualty with his head extended. Open your mouth wide, take a deep breath, and seal your lips widely on the casualty's face around the nose. Make sure your lips do not obstruct his nostrils. Close the mouth by placing your thumb on his lower lip.

If the head is not sufficiently extended, the soft palate will allow inflation through the nose but may prevent expiration. If this happens, press the casualty's lips with your thumb after each inflation.

Obstruction in the air passages

7. If efforts to inflate the lungs by mouth-to-mouth or mouth-to-nose methods fail, make sure that there is no obstruction in the mouth or throat. If a foreign body or other obstruction is found, remove it (turning his head to one side if necessary), then restart inflation.

If the obstruction is thought to be in the windpipe, in the case of:

(a) An infant or young child—lay the child prone with his head downwards over the knee and give three or four sharp slaps between the shoulders to dislodge the foreign body (Fig. 8), or hold the child up by his legs and then smack him smartly three or for times between the shoulders.

(b) An adult—turn the casualty on his side and strike him three four sharp blows between the shoulders. Check if any debris has come into the throat by feeling with the fingers. If seen remove it and start inflating again.

External cardiac resuscitation

8. The value of Respiratory Resuscitation is greatly reduced.

Oxygen cannot be carried rapidly by the circulation of blood to the brain. Should the heart cease to function it is essential that external cardiac resuscitation (an immediate method of restarting the circulation) be combined with respiratory resuscitation. It is possible that this will cause the heart to function. In some cases, external cardiac resuscitation will have to be continued until the casualty reaches hospital.

External cardiac resuscitation is not without its dangers and a first aider should only use this technique if he is sure that the heart is not functioning.

It is an advantage if two first aiders are present, one to undertake respiratory resuscitation and the other to carry out external cardiac resuscitation, working alternately.

Method

If the casualty is not breathing, mouth-to mouth or mouth-to-nose resuscitation must be performed. If after ten to twelve breaths into the casualty's lungs there is no apparent change in his condition, such as improvement in the colour of the skin, lips, or conjuctive, feel for the pulse in the neck (at the carotid pressure point). If there is no pulse external cardiac resuscitation should be started.

While continuing mouth-to mouth (or-to-nose) resuscitation the casualty should, if possible, be placed on a firm surface such as the floor, the ground, or a table. Feel the chest and locate the lower half of the sternum. In the case of:

(a) An infant or young child—with two fingers on the lower half of the sternum apply quickly six to eight sharp but not violent presses at the rate of one per second between each inflation.

(b) An adult—having located the lower half of the sternum, place the ball of the hand on it with the second hand covering the first. After each inflation of the lungs apply six to eight sharp presses at the rate of one per second.

If there are two first aiders available the person at the head should be able to feel a pulse in the neck with each pressure by the other on the sternum. He should also check this pulse periodically to see if the heart has resumed its normal beat. If so, external cardiac resuscitation should stop, but respiratory resuscitation should be continued, if necessary.

First aiders should practise on each other to feel the neck pulse at the carotid point and the position of the lower half of the sternum.

The revised silvester (chest pressure-arm lift)

METHOD OF RESPIRATORY RESUSCITATION

This manual method can be combined, if necessary, with external cardiac resuscitation.

1. If there is any obvious obstruction to breathing, remove it with your fingers or with a cloth wrapped round your fingers if it is in the mouth. Several sharp blows between the shoulder-blades may help to dislodge an obstruction.
2. Lay the casualty on his back, put something under his shoulders to raise them, and allow his head to fall backwards. The head should if possible be a little lower than the trunk. Remember that speed is essential.
3. Kneel at the casualty's head and grasp his arms at the wrists. Then cross them and press them firmly over the lower chest. This movement should force air out of his lungs.
4. Release this pressure and pull his arms with a sweeping movement upwards and outwards above his head and backwards as far as possible. This movement should cause air to be drawn into his lungs.
5. Repeat these movements rhythmically about 12 times per minute, checking the

mouth frequently for obstruction. Each cycle therefore takes five seconds -two seconds for chest pressure and three seconds for arm lift.

With the casualty on his back, there is danger of aspiration of vomit, mucus or blood. This risk can be reduced by keeping his head extended and a little lower than the trunk.

Colour Therapy

Colour therapy is based on the principle that when the body is subjected to strain, there is an alteration in the functions of somatic vibrations. The solution is to strike a balance which would make it return to the right frequency. This treatment is based on the rainbow spectrum (which consists of 12 colours). Each colour consists of different elements and minerals. This system enables you to replenish the minerals and elements that your body lacks by intake of colours that contain those minerals. Given below is the mineral and element list of various colours.

Red is composed of the gases hydrogen, cadmium, krypton and neon. Red energizes the liver, builds haemoglobin. Being a senory stimulant, it can also be an irritant. The liver, seen as the seat of emotion, needs a boost of red when a person receives a shock of any sort. Eating beetroot can help restore the balance.

Orange is good for the lungs. Preponderated by aluminium, it works as a respiratory stimulant. It depresses the parathyroid and stimulates the thyroid gland. Its silicon content makes it work as an aromatic and xenon makes it a lung builder. Eating orange coloured foods can help strengthen the respiratory system. The intake can be combined with exposure to orange light and wearing pearls, which are said to radiate orange colour.

Yellow is a motor stimulant because of its carbon content. Sodium works as a digestant and other elements in yellow can strengthen your nerves.

Gold activates the thymus gland, what this system believes to be the source of energy. So wearing the metal next to your skin improves your vitality. You can soak a gold ring or any other gold article in a glass of water, place it in the sun for a while and then drink the water.

Green stimulates the pituitary gland and its chlorine content makes it a disinfectant. It is also known to have purificatory and antiseptic properties. The radium in green makes it a muscle and a tissue builder.

Turquoise contains zinc and tantalum, which work as skin builders. Burns when exposed to turquoise light heal faster. On the other hand, its chromium content makes it a cerebral depressant.

Blue works as a cooling agent. Blue induces perspiration. Feeling itchy? It's blue you need. The colour blue works as a pain killer and a softening, soothing agent.

Scarlet—Imagine sitting in a scarlet room, dressed in scarlet robes, sinking your teeth into squashy tomatoes. Besides making your head spin, what do you think this colour will do for you? It increases your blood pressure. Scarlet works on the kidneys, its dysprosprum content being a renal energiser. The colour is also an aphrodisiac and builds sex drive.

Food Poisoning
Symptoms

Abdominal cramps, starting from an hour to 4 hours after eating tainted food and lasting up to 4 days, usually indicate bacterial food poisoning.

Abdominal cramps, headache, fever and chills, beginning from 12 to 48 hours after eating the contaminated food particularly seafood usually indicates viral food poisoning.

Sweating, dizziness, tearing in the eyes, excessive salivation, mental confusion and stomach pain beginning about 30 minutes after eating contaminated food are typical indication of chemical food poisoning. Food poisoning needs immediate attention of the doctor if there is partial loss of speech or vision and muscle paralysis, as it may be botulism poisoning. It is a life threatening illness. If the vomiting or diarrhoea is severe and lasts for more than 2 days, it's best to consult the doctor.

Treatment

a) Vomiting and diarrhoea are the body's way of flushing poison out of the system.
b) No solid food or milk should be eaten until the diarrhoea and vomiting has stopped.
c) Drink plenty of clear fluids to avoid dehydration.
d) Once you can retain the fluid in your stomach drink clear liquid.
e) Then eat bland foods like rice, cooked cereals and clear soups for a full day. If diarrhoea and vomiting is severe or prolonged, intravenous fluid may have to be taken to the hospital.
f) If your symptoms last beyond 2 days getting your stool, blood or vomited material tested can help to identify the cause of your illness.
g) Chemical food poisoning can usually be diagnosed by the description of symptoms and by testing the food potentially responsible for the poisoning.

Precautions

Never use food from containers that are leaking, bulging or damaged.

Clean utensils and cutting boards thoroughly with soap and hot water after preparing meat.

Wash fresh fruit and vegetables in cold, running water.

Store raw meat away from all other types of food.

Keep the egg dishes in the refrigerator.

Don't eat any food that looks or smells spoiled.

Avoid keeping the food near the doors, under the rotating fans or direct sunlight, to prevent the temperature changes.

Sterilise the food properly before storing it. Canned goods, especially home canned food products can harbor bacteria that need no oxygen to multiply and is not destroyed while cooking. To preserve food, sterile it in a pressure.

Thaw frozen meat or poultry completely before you cook it.

Always wash your hands before touching any food, especially after handling the raw meat.

Eat meat as soon as it is cooked. Cover up left-overs; cool, refrigerate within 90 minutes.

Store fish in the coldest part of the refrigerator.

Reheat meat quickly and thoroughly.

Foods that Will Fight Cancer

Oncologists and cancer researchers are quite firm in their opinion that certain foods have the capacity to fight cancer. From the garam masala found in the Indian spice collection to broactive compounds-enriched vegetables such as cabbage and cauliflower. Exposure to the wrong food can be carcinogenic.' According to the World Cancer Research Fund, nearly 30 to 40 percent of all cancers have a link with the food we eat, our physical activity and our weight control. And when these diet and lifestyle preferences are combined with the absence of smoking and chewing tobacco and paan, as much as 60 to 70 percent of all cancers can be prevented.

The best way to prevent cancer is to have salads, fruits and vegetables, nuts and sprouts or a natural low fat diet. Diets high in vegetable and fruits and the intake of foods rich in broactive compounds may trigger detoxification enzymes which in turn reduce the exposure of DNA to carcinogens.

Antioxidants in carrots include alpha-carotene and beta-carotene.

The indoles in cauliflower promote the production of enzymes that make the hormone estrogen less effective, reducing the risk of breast cancer.

Caffiec acid in apples increases the production of enzymes that make carcinogens more soluble in water and ultimately ejects them from the body.

Grapes contain ellagic acid, scavenger of carcinogens.

Ginger has mechanisms that suppress the creation of dangerous adducts, formed by the reaction of chemical carcinogens with DNA.

Terpenes in oranges may prevent lung cancer; while beta cryptoxanthin is an anti-cancer carotenoid.

The phytochemical phenethyl isothio-cyante in cabbage, in turnips, hampers the development of lung cancer.

Allium vegetables like garlic contain organosulphides that lower the risk of gastrointestinal cancers.

Alcohol may promote cancer. Excessive drinking can cause cancers of mouth, throat, oesophagus and liver. However, wine contains resveratol, a protective chemical.

Tomatoes get their colour from lycopene, which neutralises cancer-causing substances. The vegetable contains an estimated 10,000 plant chemicals. Ten servings a week may help reduce risk of prostate cancer by half.

Water

Water forms one of the essential components of our body. It is indispensable for our survival. However, if the water is not purified properly it can cause more harm than good. Here are a few facts about water:

Water contains three types of impurities:

Physical impurities—such as mud, dirt, soot, filth, riffraff and other dust particles which can be easily seen by the naked eye.

Chemical impurities—invisible organic salts that smell bad, and add a bad taste and colour to the water.

Germs—disease causing bacteria and viruses, which are again invisible to the naked eye. It is these impurities which are highly responsible for all kinds of water-borne diseases.

Methods of filtering

Membrane/cloth filtration: Method can remove only the physical impurities.

Candle water filters: Can remove germs and physical impurities. However with the accumulation of organic growth inside the candle pores, within a very short time, the candle easily becomes a breeding ground for disease causing germs.

Vaccum filtration: This eliminates only physical impurities. It adds an unpleasant taste to the water.

Boiling: Boiled water can be totally safe only when it is boiled continuously for 15 minutes after reaching the boiling point. But subsequent cooling and handling often leads to recontamination. Moreover, certain essential elements present in the water are either destroyed or broken down while boiling. Besides, boiling also alters the natural taste.

These days many companies offer water purifiers which solve all these problems.

Everyone is aware that boiling water destroys harmful bacteria and viruses. However, what is not known to all is the actual length of time for which the water is to be boiled.

Most people put off the gas as soon as water starts boiling. This is absolutely wrong. To make water 100% safe, it should be boiled for a full 20 minutes. This means that the time should be noted when the water starts boiling. Switch off the gas only 20 minutes after this point. Many micro-organisms do not get killed if the water is not boiled for 15-20 minutes.

The greatest loss in cooking is discarding the water after boiling the vegetables. All minerals, sugars, vitamin C, and vitamin B complex can pass out of cell walls of food into water even when food is simply cut and kept in water. Further, when these fruits/vegetables are cooked the cell walls break down.

Therefore, other nutrients which do not naturally dissolve in water pass into the cooking liquid. Hence the cooking liquid should never be thrown away. There are nutrients which dissolve in water but do not get destroyed by heat. So it is the cooking water which acts like a tonic and should be used in soups, etc.

CHAPTER-3

Personal Grooming

In an increasingly fashion conscious world, grooming has become essential for both men and women. An individual today should be aware of his/her own worth, send out right signals and make the most of him/herself. With a little bit of effort one can easily bring about a role reversal and be at the receiving end of those admiring looks.

Exercise

Do not be put off with the term exercise. Women get their fair share of exercise doing housework, but the advantage of doing specific exercises are many. Regularity in exercising is more important than anything else. For instance if you go for a half-an-hour walk everyday, it is better than doing vigorous exercises once a week or less. Similarly, do a few specific yogasanas regularly, and feel the difference. By exercise, one does not mean anything fancy like dance aerobics or going to the gym for a workout. You will be amazed at how many calories you can burn off by just changing your way of sitting, walking and doing ordinary chores.

Calories

What on earth are calories? They are nothing but the amount of energy produced by the food you eat. Though generally, every calorie is supposed to produce energy, there are some calories that do not produce any energy and are hence called empty calories. Refined sugar and high cream desserts fall into this category. These foods produce calories that get accumulated in the body as fat when consumed in excess. In short, you can avoid them, with no loss of energy.

The calories you consume every day should be in proportion to your level of physical activity. For instance if you do not do any physical work at home and also hold a desk job, the calories you expend per day are reduced very much, thereby making extra calories turn into fat that shows up in your waistline, hips, arms and thighs. Likewise, if you do a lot of physical work, the calories spent by you will be more. If you reduce them, you may feel weak and tired.

This chart only provides an approximate estimate of the ideal weight, since it can vary a little depending upon your build: whether you are a large, medium or small built person. An honest look at yourself in the mirror will tell you all you need to know.

How many calories do you need?

As explained earlier, the calories you require depend upon your activities or lack of them. On an average, though, the following chart is a good guide.

The wide variation is to allow for difference in the level of activities. You can assume that you require only the minimum calories if you do not do any vigorous housework or even exert yourself while doing the chores. A lot of bending, pushing and pulling of furniture, carrying heavy shopping up the stairs, walking up and down stairs at least two three times a day, briskly, all qualify as some form of exercise.

Which type of calories do you need?

Our food consists of three broad food types: carbohydrates, proteins and fats. Unless the food combines all the three in the right quantities, your meal will not be a balanced one and provide you the right type and number of calories you require.

Carbohydrates are required for providing energy to the body. They are the fastest to leave the stomach, since they are quickly broken down into glucose to provide energy. Rice, bread, potatoes, refined sugar and sweets are some carbohydrate foods.

Proteins are necessary for the growth and repair of cells in the body. They are present in dals, whole pulses like rajma and chana, eggs and meat.

Fats are high sources of energy and therefore, one must be very careful of the quantity one consumes. This is because, unless the person eating a high-fat diet is extremely active physically, the excess fat tends to get accumulated in the body, especially around the tummy and hips. Butter, oils, ghee, cheese and other milk products are some forms of fats. For an average adult, the maximum fat requirement per day can be about 10 gms including cooking fats.

Plan your diet to suit your calorie requirement

This may require some effort on your part, but having a food-calorie chart and planning the menu accordingly is a sensible way of losing or maintaining weight. Combine and discard food groups from this chart and you can achieve a balanced diet for your level of activity.

All vegetables have relatively fewer calories. They are highly fibrous and therefore necessary for digestion. Sweet potato is one root vegetable that is very high on calories. It provides 120 calories per 100 gms. Potato provides 94 calories. So when these are combined with fats like oil or cream and butter, their fat content goes up very high. Similarly, among fruits, banana (153 calories) chikkoo or sapota (94 calories) and mangoes (80 calories) are the high calories fruits. Watermelon (tarbuz) and white melon (kharbuj) are among the lowest calorie fruits.

Things to remember while dieting

- Note that the oil allowed for the whole day is about 2 tsps. only. Reduce salt intake since fresh vegetables and fruits have a lot of natural salt in them. Rest assured that you will not suffer from any deficiency or weakness due to less salt. According to several studies, the amount of salt a person requires in a whole day is as low as 3 gms, provided he or she consumes a lot of fresh fruits and vegetables.
- Remember to take at least 8 glasses of water in a day.
- Never drink water during the meals. However, if a large appetite is a problem with you and you tend to overeat, sip a glass of hot water half an hour before the meal.
- Chew each mouthful slowly and do not gulp down the food or wash it down with cold drinks or water. The process of digestion is upset by this method.
- According to studies, a person feels satiated 20 minutes after eating food.

So it is important to make each mouthful last by chewing thoroughly and eating for at least 20-25 minutes. This will prevent the urge to snack after a meal.

- Avoid pickles and sauces since these contain preservatives and high quantities of salt, both of which are bad for dieters.
- Do not go on fad diets, like an all fruit or all milk diet. Also, never eat unappetising food thinking that it will help you reduce. Chances are, you will put the weight you may lose double fast once you go back to your original diet. There is also the danger of deficiencies and sudden collapse.
- Slimming concoctions and pills are best avoided because their efficacy is not proven.
- Exercise is very important. Set aside at least 15 minutes a day for some form of exercise—walking, yogasana, skipping, etc.
- When you go for parties, have something at home to take the edge off the hunger. Try to stick to salads and vegetables as far as possible. Avoid the sweet dish or go in for fruits if there are.
- If you are planning to lose weight, think in terms of vegetarian food and that too simple dishes that do not require too much frying. Meats if you must take, should be lean (fat removed) and boiled as far as possible. Western cooking is best in this respect.

Myths about dieting

Eating less will **not** make you lose weight. I know of women who literally starve to become thinner, but find themselves getting fatter. Even if you do, you will regain it soon. Exercising is a better way to lose weight.

Not all the calories are the same. calories from carbohydrate foods like whole wheat bread (roti, brown bread), boiled or baked potatoes, pasta, etc. are burned for energy. But excess fats get stored in the body.

Starches are **not fattening**. But if you add fats like oil, ghee or butter, cream, etc. it will add to the calories and turn fattening. For example, potatoes when plain boiled or baked is a good source of energy, but when fried, turns fattening. Making parathas in vanaspati or ghee is also the same.

The most difficult task that faces a dieter is eating out. It is here that he loses the battle of the bulge. However, occasional treats are not harmful to healthy eating habits. It is better to eat in small quantities foods that you crave, e.g chocolates, rather than allowing build up to unmanageable heights. Here are a few choices you can make at a restaurant:

Healthy eating habits should be inculcated as early as possible. Here are a few suggestions for a healthy diet for children:

a) Make use of non-stick cooking utensils to reduce fat while cooking.

b) Use vegetable oils for cooking instead of ghee or butter.

c) Increase their consumption of high fibre whole grain cereals such as whole wheat flours, brown rice and potatoes. Use a mixture of whole meal and white flours for baking cakes for young children.

d) Make all the changes gradually.

e) Eat food which is as near to the natural state as possible, avoiding foods with artificial additives and colours.

f) It is not necessary for children to have large amounts of potato wafers, chocolates and sweets in the lunch box. Try to avoid sugary or fried snacks as they destroy appetite, but a fruit or salad to chew on is a good idea.

g) By weaning children straight on to the healthy diet that is great fun. Your kids will enjoy it as much as you do. And before you know it, you have prepared the foundation which will ultimately set your child in good stead for a healthy life in the future. They will be free from modern day scourges of poor dietary habits and poor nutrition.

Although the problem of over-weight people has been addressed widely, those who are underweight rarely find material on how to put on weight. Here are a few tips:

a) Eat a balanced meal which is slightly high in calories.
b) Concentrate on workouts to tone your body and build muscles.
c) Remember that weight gain should be slow. Sudden weight fluctuations cause immense harm to the body.

A few more tips for a healthy life

Give attention to your hand, feet, nails.

Weight is not a criteria to judge your fitness. It is a free fat percentage.

Do not take any food for 1/2 hour before exercising.

No food is fattening; it is either too much or too little.

Fat is equally essential in the diet as Vitamin A, D, E and K is absorbed through fat only.

After 30 years of age, exercise is must for calcium deposition in bone, otherwise osteoporosis sets in.

As eyes are the mirror of your face, skin is the mirror of your health.

Vitamin C increases your body response and is available in plenty amount in Amla, Guava, Lemon.

Roughage should be the important part of your diet and it is found in whole grains, fruits and vegetables.

Laughter is the best medicine as it exercises all the muscles of your body in a positive direction.

Fresh fruits and vegetables are the main source of vitamins and minerals.

Dieting doesn't mean starvation it means balanced diet.

Balanced diet means combination of carbohydrates, proteins, fat, vitamins, minerals and plenty of water.

As calcium and phosphorus are main minerals for bone formation, iron and zinc are main minerals for blood formation.

Losing weight through starvation leads to many medical complication like anaemia, low blood pressure, weakness and giddiness.

To keep your skin glowing use choker, kacha *dudh* and *haldi* instead of soap.

Massage

Massage should be applied at such regular daily time as suits the mutual convenience of patient and operator. The purpose of massage is to increase and perfect nutritive activity in special designated parts, which implies unequal distribution of its processes.

The commencing processes should usually be at the extremities, more frequently the lower.

The degree of force of the processes applied must be apportioned to the degrees of irritability of the different parts of the body, and must be greatest to the least irritable parts. Sensitiveness to impressions is an approximate measure of irritability. With the processes properly adjusted, the irritability and liability to local pain disappears as the local diseased organs are approached, and no other than agreeable sensations are evoked by the processes.

An hour or two spent in the application of the processes, with their intervals, is quite sure to superinduce a feeling of, and a desire for, repose, which often culminates in sound sleep.

Good Posture

Whatever your height, walk straight and tall. One way to do this is to imagine someone pulling you up with strings from your shoulders. Slouching will not only make you look shorter but also make your shoulders look round and your neck sunken. Square your shoulders, look straight and you would have added inches to your height. Good posture also makes you feel more confident.

The right sitting posture

Make it a habit to sit with a straight back. This may sound difficult and to begin with, you may sit with drooping shoulders, but if you remember to straighten your shoulders and back, soon, you will find yourself improving your posture. This is very important for people who have a desk job or do a lot of work on the computer or typewriter. You will actually find back pain reducing, by sitting straight. If you do not believe me, try this. Sit slouched at the table for 15 minutes and then straighten your

back and shoulders. The nagging pain in the back will reduce. If it returns again, it means that you have slouched again!

When you are simply sitting, say, at the doctor's, do not fidget while standing or sitting. Fold your hands on your lap if you are sitting. If you feel restless, you can always hold a book or newspaper or even knit. Cracking fingers, biting nails and fiddling with the hair, are all signs of agitation and best avoided.

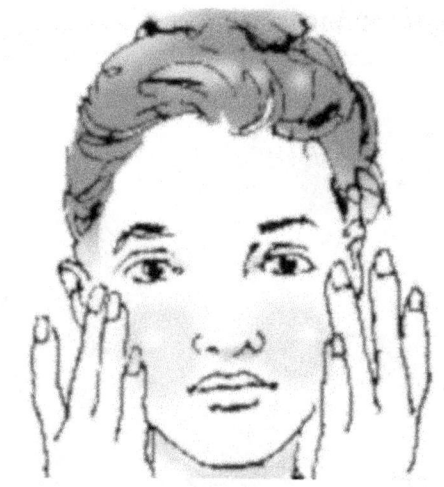

Some ideas for a better posture

You cannot help how tall or short you are, but you certainly can try and **appear** tall and well proportioned, with the help of dress, make-up and accessories like shoes and jewellery. It is not difficult to make a thin person appear fatter, a fat person to look thinner and so on.

Skin Care

Find out your skin type

Before you pick a skincare regime it is important to know what your skin type is.

Oily Skin feels greasy on the surface and is prone to breakouts and blemishes, enlarged pores and a constant shine.

Normal skin is soft and supple with a smooth feel.

Dry skin appears dull and flaky. It is also likely to feel tight and rough after being outdoors.

Combination skin looks patchy— some areas look oily and some dry e.g. the forehead, nose and chin known as the "T-Zone" appear oily and shiny while the skin on the cheeks are dry.

Skin routine for different skin types

CLEANSING - TONING

Teenage: Clean your face regularly and use a sunscreen lotion during the day.

If you are prone to pimples, get a dermi-check and follow the routine for oily skin.

Clean your face of all dirt and make-up every night before sleeping.

Get into a regular skincare routine that is suited to your skin type and always handle your skin very gently.

20s: Check your skin for superficial fine lines and wrinkles. Use moisturisers regularly.

A sunscreen is a must for daily use.

By now you should be following a regular skincare routine.

This is the age where you experiment with make-up, so cleanse off all make-up thoroughly.

30-40: Check your skin for superficial fine lines, wrinkles and sagging skin.

Visits to a beauty therapist for facials is advisable.

Follow a regular skincare routine and add on a Skin Replenishing Night Cream or Skin Revival Lotion/System to your regular moisturiser.

40-50: During these years your skin needs extra care since a lot of skin changes occur, e.g. change of skin type from oily to dry or vice-versa, breaking out into pimples, sudden sagging around the jaw line, wrinkles due to sun damage in the earlier years.

Keep a watch on your skin, and visit a beauty therapist if required.

50s and beyond: Normally skin tends to get drier after 50 and needs a lot of nourishing and moisturising for which Skin Revival Lotion/System is ideal.

Facial

Facial is a process of complete cleansing, toning and tightening the facial skin and muscles. If you have the time, you could go to a beauty parlour, but having a facial at home is not at all difficult. You do not even require fancy equipment for it. You will need:

1. A big bowl of boiling water
2. Cold cream or olive oil
3. Face pack
4. Lots of cotton
5. A little rose water
6. An astringent lotion

First of all, start with creaming your face. Take generous quantities of cold cream and apply over the face and neck, massaging it well into the skin. While massaging, use upwards strokes. Massage around the eyes and between the eyes using upward and outward strokes. While doing the neck, use a downward motion. Massage for at least 10 minutes.

Wet a piece of cotton and remove all the grime and dust from the massaged areas. Boil a large bowl of water. Bring it to a table. Bend your face over it, with a thick towel covering your face and head to keep in the steam. Stay like that till the water becomes warm. By now, your face would have begun to "sweat". Lightly dab with some cotton.

Next, remove the blackheads and tweeze the eyebrows.

Do not use soap or any other cosmetic on the face for at least 12 hours, to allow the skin to breathe.

Go to a beauty parlour at least once every two or three months to get a professional facial. Keeping your skin clean with home facials is a good idea, even if you do go to the parlour.

When you have absolutely no time, you can quickly steam the face and wipe well with cotton to remove the dirt and grime.

Blackheads and whiteheads

These are impurities that enter the skin through the pores and get settled. Generally, oily skins are more prone to blackheads and the nose and forehead are the main areas where these are found. By steaming the face, these can be loosened, since the pores get enlarged. Use a blackhead remover to gently remove these from the face. Be careful to avoid injury. Never try to squeeze them out with your nails since they may get infected that way.

Face packs

DRY SKIN

1. Mix the yolk of one egg with a teaspoonful of almond oil, adding the oil drop by drop to the yolk, and stirring constantly. Apply to the face and neck and leave for 15 to 20 minutes. Remove with warm water.
2. Add olive oil drop by drop to two tablespoons of white flour (maida) until it is the consistency of a soft porridge. This pack should be kept on for half an hour if possible. Remove with rain water or rose water.
3. Mix one tablespoon of pure butter or ghee with half a tablespoon of cocoa. Leave on the skin for 15 minutes. This pack does not have a very pleasant smell, but has a wonderfully softening effect. Remove with warm water and soap.

NORMAL SKIN

1. Boil two tablespoons of white flour with milk to make a soft consistency. Add a little rose water and spread over the face and neck while warm (not hot). Leave on for 15 minutes. Remove with warm water.
2. Mix some whole wheat flour (atta) with a little water. Cook on a low heat for about 5 minutes, stirring all the time. Add one teaspoon of honey and mix well. The pack should have a soft, porridge-like consistency and should be applied to the face while still warm. Leave it on for 15 to 20 minutes. Remove with warm water and soap.
3. To one teaspoonful of honey, add a few drops of almond oil. Spread all over the face and neck. Leave for ten minutes, then remove with rain or softened water. This pack has an excellent softening effect and is especially useful for removing fine wrinkles.

OILY SKIN

1. Mix together equal parts of cornflour and talcum powder. Add a little cold water and mix until the pack has the consistency of soft porridge. Spread over the face and neck and leave for 20 minutes. Remove with cotton wool which has been soaked in astringent lotion.
2. Beat the white of an egg until it is quite stiff. Spread lightly over the face. Leave till dry, then remove with astringent lotion.
3. Grate some cucumber (Kheera), add a few drops of lime juice and a teaspoonful of rose water. Place between two pieces of gauze or fine cloth and apply to the face. Leave for 15 to 20 minutes.

It is important to remember that face packs should not be left on the skin for more than the stipulated time. And never apply a pack to the fine skin under the eyes.

Each skin type needs different care

DRY SKIN

Cleanse: Give up washing your face in soap and water for a while, and cleanse your skin with cold cream or cleansing milk only. After a week or two of this treatment, you may wash your face with soap and warm water, but only just once a day, preferably at night before your skin care routine. At other times during the day you may cleanse your face with cream or cleansing milk, and after doing this you may splash your face with cool water to give you a fresh feeling.

Tone: Immediately after cleansing, tone your skin. Take a small piece of cotton wool, soak it in water, wring it out and moisten with a little skin tonic. Pat gently all over your face and neck. Do not apply to the skin under your eyes.

Nourish: A dry skin needs plenty of oil, as an over-dry one inevitably leads to premature wrinkles. There are plenty of expensive skin foods for women with dry skin, but there is no need to spend a great deal of money. Nothing can rival almond oil for improving dry skin. Apply it lightly, using upward and outward strokes. Using the third finger of your left hand, pat it in very gently under the eyes.

Normal skin

Cleanse: First wash your face with soap and water, then give it a thorough cleansing with cleansing milk.

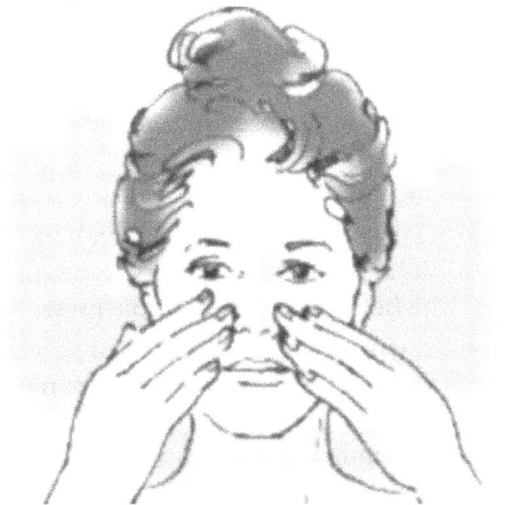

Tone: Your skin with skin tonic (rose water is fine for this purpose) or a mild astringent lotion. Apply the tonic or lotion with a small piece of cotton wool. Pat it into the skin: don't rub. Do not apply to the skin under your eyes.

Nourish: A nightly application of almond oil is very effective in guarding against wrinkles and for nourishing the skin. However, if your skin shows signs of becoming oily after starting this treatment, stop it immediately and nourish with a light cream instead.

Oily skin

Cleanse: Soap and water is ideal for a greasy skin. Wash your face as often as possible—three or four times a day-using a medicated soap. Never use cold cream for deep cleansing. You should, of course, use a cleansing milk, for soap and water alone can not penetrate into the pores to clean away every trace of grime and stale make-up. But remember to rinse your face in tepid water after using cleansing milk.

Tone: Your skin with a good astringent lotion (see Astringent).

Nourish: Nourishing the skin means replenishing the natural oils that are lost during the day and when the face is washed. Since your skin is already oily, you will not need to do this. However, as you get older you may, if you wish, use a reliable hormone cream with a non-greasy base.

If you have "combination" skin

Some women have "combination" skin. This means that part of the face is one skin type, part another. For example, someone with a predominantly dry skin may have an oily patch down the centre of her face. Another woman may have greasy skin with a dry patch on her chin or forehead. If you have "combination" skin treat the different parts of your face according to type.

Fruits and their use

Oranges: Orange juice makes a fine skin tonic. Dip a piece of cotton wool in equal parts of orange juice and water. Dab it on all over face and neck.

Water melon: Water melon has been described as "nature's own moisturizer". Cut off large, thin slices from the fruit and lay them over your face and neck. Leave for about 20 minutes.

Grapes: Mix the juice of ripe grapes with half the amount of rose water. Use as a skin tonic.

Tomatoes: Boil some ripe tomatoes in a little water. Strain the liquid and use it to wash your face.

Peaches: Grate the fruit finely and place between two layers of fine cloth. Now place the compress over your face and leave for 20 minutes. If possible, chill the compress slightly before use.

Strawberries: Cut a big strawberry in half. Rub the cut side of the fruit all over your face and neck.

Bananas: Mash a ripe banana. Mix with two tablespoons of wheat flour and spread all over your face and neck.

Hair

It is rightly called the crowning glory of a woman. You need to pay a lot of attention to it. The foremost rule of hair care is to keep it scrupulously clean. Shampoo at least once a week if the weather is cold and twice if it is warm. Hair tends to collect a lot of dust and grime due to the pollution in the air and the sweat on the scalp. When it becomes dirty, it sticks to the scalp and looks dull and flat.

Hair facts

- Having your hair swinging glossily over your shoulders is a very sensual image. But only well-conditioned hair does this. In fact, long hair alters a woman's whole body language.

- Knowing when to stop: Long hair like short hair, needs regular trimming to look its absolute best.
- Knowing what suits you: Long hair can be ageing. Those who have long or thin faces, in particular, should avoid growing their hair long.
- Its colour: Brown and black hair are thickest and grow the longest;
- Hair grows at the rate of 2.5 cm in a month-until it gets to 25 cm long, when it slows down to 1.25 cm. Hair oil in itself does not make your hair grow. A good oil massage makes the oil reach the hair roots, thus inducing growth and general conditioning.
- Hair colours cannot grey your hair. They don't reach the roots and hence cannot be held responsible for the greys.
- You must keep changing your shampoo from time to time. Hair conditions keep changing - oily in summer and dry in winter - and you need to treat this change accordingly.

- Remember that wet hair is extra-delicate: Use a wide-toothed comb to detangle.
- Stimulate blood circulation by massaging your scalp and brushing well (but not too often). The better the blood circulation, the better your hair.
- Sun and wind wreck hair condition. What you need is protection for hair from dehydration, splitting and fading.

Shampoo and conditioner

Use a good shampoo that has conditioner in it, though you can also use an ordinary shampoo and use a conditioner separately. Nowadays you can buy a lot of different varieties which have herbal ingredients.

If you have the time and energy, you can go in for purely natural ingredients like *shikakai, amla, hibiscus* leaves and flowers, tulsi etc. Otherwise choose from among the various types of shampoos available—for dry, oily and normal hair.

Home-made shampoo powder

100 gms shikakai

50 gms hibiscus leaves (dried in the shade)

1 tsp *methi* seeds

4 or 5 dried lemon rinds (halves)

2 tsp. dried amla

Dry these well in the sun (except hibiscus) and powder finely. Store in an airtight jar. When required, take a teaspoonful or more, mix with a little water to make a paste and apply on hair. Work up a lather. (The hibiscus leaves are foamy and act like soap.) Wash after 5 minutes. This powder not only cleans, but also conditions the hair. The methi is good for treating dandruff and has a cooling effect.

Is oil necessary for your hair?

Oil is cooling for the scalp and it also protects the hair from harsh chemicals in the shampoos. It is therefore very essential to massage your scalp with warm oil before shampooing. You can use any one of the following oils: Olive oil, coconut oil or til oil. Mustard oil may be massaged if you can bear the strong smell.

Take a few drops and massage with the fingertips well into the scalp using gentle circular motion. This way the blood circulation of the scalp is restored and aids hair growth. You do not need cupfuls of oil for your hair. In fact your hair does not need it at all.

Oily hair makes your hair look plastered on and also collects a lot of dust and grime.

In order to make the oil massage more effective, you can take steam treatment. Wrap a towel dipped in hot water on the head after the oil massage. Check the temperature by holding the towel against the back of the hand. It should be bearable, or else, there are chances of your getting burnt. When the towel cools, use another towel. Alternate the two towels for about 15 to 20 minutes. Shampoo immediately.

This treatment leaves your hair well conditioned and helps remove dandruff too, if done regularly.

Shampooing

Ensuring that hair is clean and shiny is the most important step in hair care. Choose a shampoo from a reputable manufacturer to suit your hair type. The active cleansing ingredients vary considerably in quality. A shampoo should cleanse thoroughly without irritating or demoisturizing the scalp. This is more important than the acid/alkali balance for an alternative view on the choice of shampoo. It should not be necessary to use much shampoo to get good results, nor should shampooing leave the hair 'squeaky clean', as this indicates that too much oil and moisture have been removed. Such additives as herbs and fruit or protein do not affect the hair's condition.

Really greasy hair may be washed once a day but it is inadvisable to shampoo more than once or twice a week if your hair is dry, as over-washing can rob the hair of moisture. Dry shampoos made of a grease-absorbing fine powder, help to make hair look fresher when there is no time to wash it.

You will need: a brush or comb with widely spaced teeth, a spray attachment, mixer tap or shower, and shampoo.

1. Brush or comb hair thoroughly to loosen dirt and dead skin cells from the scalp. Wet the hair with the spray, so the underneath layers are saturated with water as well as the top ones.
2. Pour a small amount, roughly a teaspoon, of shampoo into the palm of the hand.
3. Massage the shampoo gently into the roots with the fingertips covering the whole of the scalp.
4. With the flat of the hand, work the shampoo into the bulk of the hair over the top layers.
5. Rinse with the spray, using lukewarm water, until every trace of shampoo has been removed. Repeat the sequence if necessary.

Dandruff

This is a scalp condition where dead cells of the scalp get flaky. It is caused by both too oily and too dry scalps which are undernourished. Dandruff can be most annoying. First of all a scalp with dandruff itches. Secondly the flakes fall all over the dress; thirdly it can turn hair lifeless and limp.

The best way to control dandruff is through proper and good nutrition. Plenty of raw vegetables and fruits and lots of buttermilk (mattha) in the diet is considered very good for healthy hair.

Use an anti-dandruff shampoo to prevent and control dandruff. Selsun is a good shampoo which when applied regularly controls dandruff.

Home made dandruff Care

Poppy seeds (khus-khus)	1 tsp.
Fenugreek seeds (methi)	1 tsp.
Peppercorns	5-6 corns.

Soak all the ingredients for one hour. Grind into a fine paste. Apply on scalp. Let it seep into the scalp for at least two hours. Wash off with warm water. Rinse well. This is a very effective remedy, but the only problem is that the methi sticks to the hair and requires a lot of patience of wash and comb out of the hair.

Another method is to shake salt from a salt cellar on the dry hair and scalp. Massage gently into the scalp. Wash off with a mild shampoo.

Grey hair

After the age of 35 hair starts turning grey. The onset of grey can be delayed or early in individual cases, depending upon various factors like heredity and health. Whatever may be the case, you need not go through life with salt and pepper hair, if you don't want to. Any number of hair-dyes are available in the market for darkening hair. Liquid dyes are the most popular. Follow instructions given in the pack.

You can make use of home preparations for dyeing hair. Henna is an effective hair darkener. Regular use of this herb will delay the greying process. When the hair is light in colour, it gives a dark reddish tint to the hair. However, if you want to avoid the red tint, use amla along with it.

You can use any of the store-bought hair dyes and follow the instructions given in it. Godrej hair dye is a good brand as is also Bigen.

Home-made dye

Take half a cup of henna powder, mix a quarter cup of amla powder and make a paste with curds. Apply this paste to the hair. Make partings close to each other and apply the paste in such a way that the roots are covered well. Coat the hair strands too. Let the dye soak for at least two hours. Wash with warm water and a mild shampoo.

Precaution

While using hair-dyes, wear rubber gloves to protect the hands. Also take care not to accidentally apply the dye on the skin since it is very difficult to remove. Wear old clothes to prevent them getting stained.

Go grey gracefully

It is certainly not compulsory for everyone to dye their hair if they grow grey. A shock of grey hair or a patch of grey can look very attractive. Do you remember the famous grey patch of Mrs. Indira Gandhi? Sometimes it may be wiser to let the grey be. Nothing can look sillier than a wrinkled face sporting a shock of jet-black hair! But dye by all means if grey makes you feel old and self-conscious.

Manicure and pedicure

These are also possible at home with a little effort and practically no expense. You require:

1. A basin of warm water each for hands and feet.
2. Some liquid soap.
3. Cotton buds.
4. Nail clipper.
5. Fleer for filing nails.
6. Hand cream.

Soak your hands and feet in the basin of warm water, to which some liquid toilet soap has been added, for at least 15 minutes. Gently knead and squeeze the muscles of the hand and feet, working off the accumulated dirt and grime.

Pat dry with a soft towel. Clip the nails of fingers and toes, cutting straight across the toe nails to prevent in- grown toenails. If you want to grow your fingernails long, shape them accordingly and file them smoothly. With the cotton buds, gently push back the cuticles of the nails. Clean the inside of the finger nails with a cotton bud. File the clipped nails with an emery board for a smooth finish.

Massage hands and feet with cream, pressing the soles of the feet and the palms as you do, to remove the tiredness and also the roughness out of them. Apply nail varnish or polish after the manicure and pedicure.

Nail polish

- Select the shade of the nail polish that will match with your dress and lipstick. Going for bright red nail polish while applying a pink or orange lipstick will clash.
- Take care to see that the toes are separate by putting small balls of cotton between the toes to prevent the nail polish from smudging. Allow to dry under a fan.
- Apply the polish in single strokes, beginning from the cuticle and going to the top of the finger/toe. Apply a second coat after the first one dries, for an even, smooth finish.

- Never scrape off old polish. Use a nail polish remover.
- Do not grow nails too long.
- Remember to keep finger nails clean. Dirt under the nails is more ugly than chipped nails.

- Nail polish comes in plain as well as frosted shades. The latter are better in terms of finish and give a pearly glow to your nail polish.
- Wear the same shade on your toes and finger nails.
- Match nail polish exactly to the of lipstick: pearl and natural shades however, can be worn with any shade of lipstick.
- Remove chipped nail polish.

Eyebrows

You can shape your brows with a tweezers or by threading. When you have very thick brows that need to be trimmed, threading is better as it is faster. It is better done by a beautician, while you can use the tweezers yourself.

- Before beginning, wipe brows with a piece of cotton soaked in Eau de Cologne.
- Stretch the skin taut with left hand and begin tweezing.
- Always tweeze by grasping as near the root of the hair as possible and pulling along the growth of the hair.
- Keep the thickness the same till you reach the arch and then slowly taper it off.
- Do not make the eyebrows longer than the end of the eyes.
- Always tweeze from below.
- Keep the natural arch at the top, as far as possible.
- If you have thin brows, use an eyebrow pencil, using short, light and feathery strokes upward and outward.
- Very thin eyebrows are out. The look is more natural nowadays. So all you may need is a few deft strokes of the tweezers.
- While tweezing eyebrows, go slow and carefully. You can tweeze an extra hair later, but you will not able to grow instant hair if you over-tweeze by mistake.

Make-up

Make-up is an art. It adds a touch of glamour to the face. It highlights your good features and helps camouflage the bad ones. However, one should keep in mind that it should look as natural as possible.

Basic requirements

PRODUCTS

- Foundation
- Under eye concealer
- Contouring brush
- Check contour
- Highlighter

- Mascara
- Lip liner
- Lipstick
- Lip gloss
- Face powder
- Eye shadow
- Eye liner

TOOLS

- A large long handled soft brush for applying blushes and powder
- A child tooth brush to brush up brow
- Slant tipped brushes for applying eye shadow
- Tapered up brush
- Brow brush angled
- Tweezers
- Pencil sharpener
- Stiff brush for applying brow contour

SUPPLIES

- Tissues
- Cotton
- Q-Tips
- Make-up sponges

What kind of a face do you have?

KNOWING YOUR FACE TYPE

Oval: The widest area will be around the eyes and ears with gradual curves towards the forehead and jawline.

Pear: Your face will be close to the vertical lines at your forehead and wider than the lines at your ears and jawline.

Square: There is same amount of your face outside the vertical sticks, all the way down the jawline.

Rectangular or oval: There is very little of your face outside the two vertical sticks, with virtually the same width top, middle and bottom.

Heart: A great deal of your forehead is visible outside the two vertical sticks, a little less at the ear area and very little if any at the jawline.

Diamond: There is very little face visible outside the two vertical sticks and this will be close to the ear area, tapering sharply towards a narrow forehead and chin area.

Round: The widest points which overlap the vertical sticks will be around the ear area with a gradual curving up to the forehead and down to the jawline, creating an almost round shape.

Step by step guide to makeup

- Start with a clean skin. It is a must to have a freshly cleaned skin before putting on any type of make up.
- Now apply a skin covering: this could be in the form of a foundation (liquid or cake) loose or pressed powder or a blusher. Foundation is the base of the make up. Carry the foundation right from the hair line down under the chin. Put it on lightly and work it into the skin until it has a sheer over all look. Remember that your foundation should match your skin shade exactly.
- For greasy skin: use liquid or pancake foundation.
- For normal or dry skin: use cream foundation. This gives a smooth matte finish.

Rouge

Should be applied next. Cream rouge for dry skin and powder rouge for oily skin should be used. Use your rouge as follows:

Square face: Place rouge down the sides of your cheeks and blend over back point of jaw bone.

Long face: Place rouge at a point under the triangle of your cheek bones and blend out no further than the corner of your eyes.

Round face: Place rouge in a long triangle at the sides of the face. The corner of the triangle should almost touch the outer corner of the eye.

Heart-shaped face: Place rouge high over your cheek bones. Sweep back and upwards towards the hair line.

Face powder

Should be exactly the same shade as your foundation. For a more translucent look choose one shade lighter than the foundation. Apply with a smooth powder puff. Brush off excess with a fluffy powder puff or a facial brush.

Lipstick

Lipstick not only gives colour and shape to the mouth, but also protects the sensitive skin of the lips from cracking in strong winds and cold.

Applying lipstick:

- First outline the lips with a lip pencil or brush. The colour should be a shade brighter and darker than the lipstick itself, with which you will 'fill in'. Remember that they should be of the same shade.
- Fill in with a soft lip brush. This is better than applying the stick directly, since the cracks are filled in and also makes the lipstick last longer.
- Let the colour set for at least three to four minutes before blotting with a tissue. Apply another coat and blot with tissue again. This will 'set' the colour properly.
- Apply lip gloss for the natural look.

HOW TO MASK DEFECTS

If lips are too thin: While drawing the outline, draw it slightly above and below the normal lip line. Fill in.

If the lower lip is too full: Draw a line inside the natural shape of the lip. Fill in and blot well.

If the mouth is very small or narrow: Extend the corners of the lips on both sides, keeping the natural shape of the mouth in mind. Fill in and blot.

- While choosing the colour of the lipstick, keep in mind your complexion. Dark skinned people should avoid using bright pinks and reds. Very bright shades are better suited for the evenings, while milder shades look good during the day. Roll on lip gloss can be used to highlight the lipstick or even used by itself, without using lipstick.
- Colour or lipstick should match the colour of Bindi worn.

Some make up hints

Receding chin: Apply highlighter across the chin line blending it under the jaw.

Double chin: Apply shadow across the lower part of the chin blending it under the jaw.

Protruding chin: Highlight the area around the mouth to make the chin look as if it is receding.

Pointed chin: Highlight both sides of the pointed chin and shade the tip.

Receding forehead: Apply highlighter straight across the forehead blending it into the hairline.

Protruding forehead: Apply shadow straight across the bulging part of the forehead and blend into the hairline.

GIVING A SHAPE TO YOUR NOSE AND BLUSHING YOUR FACE

Nose type:

Prominent: Apply highlighter starting from either side of the nose and extending just beneath the middle of the eye. This will make the nose appear to recede, thereby making it less conspicuous.

Short: To give illusion of greater length, apply highlighter straight down the centre from the bridge of the nose to under the tip. Pluck eyebrows to give a wider space between them and a longer line to the nose.

Curved: Apply shadow to the high point of the curve, then carefully blend highlighter both above and below the shadowed area.

Upturned: Apply highlighter straight down the centre from the bridge of the nose to under the tip, then shadow the turned up portion and blend downwards.

Broad: To make the nose appear narrow in width, highlight down the centre from the bridge to the tip, then shadow on either side to create a "diamond" pattern of correction.

Protruding: Shadow down the length of the bridge and highlight on either side. Be careful not to bring the highlighter over the nostrils.

Long: To cut down the apparent length of a nose apply shadow on the tip, blending it under the nose.

BLUSHING THE FACE

Face type:

Oval: Apply blusher high on the cheek bones in a triangular shape, and blend into the hairline.

Round: Apply blusher in a wide triangular pattern, blending into the hairline and over the earlobe.

Diamond: Apply blusher in a wedge-like pattern on the highest point of the cheekbone, being careful not to blend the blusher into the hollow of the cheeks.

Rectangular: Apply blusher to the cheekbone in a rectangular pattern, keeping it very narrow. Do not run the blusher down the length of the face.

Pear: Apply blusher in a wide triangular pattern. Do not blend the blusher close to the nose area.

Heart: Apply blusher in a narrow wedge-like pattern on the highest point of the cheek bone.

Square: Create a triangular pattern on the cheekbone. Blend downwards over the earlobe.

Eye make up

Eye brow contouring: is applied first. Keep the line of the brow subtle and graceful. If your eyebrows are scanty or fair, emphasize them with a dark brown or black pencil used in short feathery strokes. Ensure that the pencil is well sharpened before use.

Eye shadow: is the next step. For day wear, one should avoid bright colours.

i) **Dark eyes:** brown, beige, green and mauve.
ii) **Blue or grey eyes:** light grey, blue or mauve.
iii) **Hazel eyes:** green and dark grey are most suitable.

The eye shadow should be blended in carefully.

Eye liner (liquid): to apply pull up the outer corner of the eye and with a quick, firm stroke outline the edge of the upper lid keeping close to the line all the way to the outer corner but not beyond it. If you have small eyes, you can continue all around the eye with the liner.

Mascara: makes the eye lashes appear thicker. Apply with quick short strokes from the base to the tip of the lashes. To make the eyes appear larger, apply mascara on both upper and lower lashes.

Handy hints

1. If you want to emphasise the eyes, you can use eyeliner on the base of the upper and lower lashes. Start from the inner eye and proceed to the outer portion, drawing a thin line.
2. Eye shadow gives the eyes a dramatic effect, especially in the evenings under artificial light. The shade used has to harmonise with the colour of the eyes, clothes and the time of the day. You can use the frosted variety for the evenings and the matte variety during the day. Highlighting with gold or silver is also reserved for the evenings. A general rule while applying eye shadow: use a colour to blend with your dress, especially if you have dark eyes.
3. If your eye colour is black or dark brown, you can use a wide variety of shades from mauve to brown.
4. While wearing eye shadow, remember that the darker shades with a touch of gold or silver are best for the night. Day make up should be simple and subtler.....

Hide flaws

To hide flaws, two shades of foundation are used: one light and the other darker. The light foundation is used to enlarge or bring forward and the darker is used to make smaller or recede. Always use darker foundation over the lighter one blending the edges well so that no dividing line is visible.

To thin down a too-round face: Use the shadow method. Use a shadow-base, orange-brown blusher or brown or charcoal grey powder eye shadow (depending on your skin tone) and brush softly down side of face, starting from just below temple to beginning of jawline. Blend in hollow of cheeks.

To play up cheekbones: Use a lighter tone of base or powder than your skin tone (white, dry eye shadow works well) and apply lightly under your cheekbone, then cover your face with your regular foundation or powder, blending very gently. Take a darker tone blusher or shadow and brush on cheekbone itself. This will mould your facial bones which can be one of your most attractive features.

To thin down or shorten nose: Use a darker shade of base or a touch of dark brown cream eye shadow and blend it along sides of your nose. Add a dab beneath tip of nose for a turned-up look.

To give wide-eyed round look to eyes: Make your liner heavier at centre of eye than at the outside corners. If Eyes Are Too Close Together: Blend a light shade of eye shadow from centre of lid to outer corner. If eyes are too far apart, apply shadow at corners of lids nearest nose.

To thin down lipline: Using a lipstick brush, draw outline slightly under your natural lipline. If mouth is too wide, concentrate the application of lipstick to the centre of it, blending lightly to the outer corners. Keep away from chalky-pastel shades.

To create a smile effect: Apply your lipstick with a smile in your mind. Translation: bring corners up and out- never turned down.

A note about highlighting and shadowing: "Highlight" means to use a lighter shade of your own skin tone on areas you wish to play up. "Shadow" means to use a darker base, powder, or blusher on areas you wish to play down.

Clothes and Jewellery

It is often said that, "clothes maketh a man". The first impression that one creates is established by the way we dress and what accessories we use. It is thus important for men and women to dress right: both for their age and the occasion. The following factors can be kept in mind:

The cut of your clothes is a vital component of dressing well.

a) **Women:** who wear western outfits should pay attention to neck lines, sleeve lengths, waist and hip detailing and the length of the skirt. If your hips are heavy, wear a stunning blouse with a comparatively sober shirt or a pair of trousers.

b) **Men:** should also choose their clothes according to their body shape.

- Those with long necks look good in mandarin collars, while those with short necks look good in buttoned down collars with pointed ends.
- Heavily built men should wear single breasted jackets while those who are underweight should wear double-breasted jackets.
- Well tonned men look good in collarless T-shirts and shirts with pleated or embroidered fronts.
- If your physique needs something to be desired, go in for sports shirt with collar.

While choosing the colour of your clothes, keep in mind your complexion.

a) **If you have a wheatish complexion:** you would look best in earth tones like olive, green, khaki, rust and mushroom.

b) Fair complexion will look good in almost any colour.

c) Make sure that the most arresting colour is worn on top or bottom, depending on which part you want to highlight.

Dress to suit the occasion. There are four broad categories though the boundaries between them can be blurred:

- Formal day wear
- Informal day wear
- Formal night wear
- Informal night wear

Keep in mind the fabric that you choose and the accessories that you choose.

Make sure that you smell good. There are many ways of combating body odour:

i) **Soap:** is vital to keep clean, however it has a short term effect and should be supplemented with other products.

ii) **Talc:** Talc works by absorbing the sweat and keeping the skin surface dry.
iii) **Perfumes/after shaves:** are essentially enhancement products that mask the body odour temporarily.
iv) **Deodorants:** are the most effective way of keeping body odour away. They should be used daily.

To choose the fragrance that is right for you, two factors are important:

a) The image you like to project
b) Your mood

The fragrance should suit and enhance your personality, e.g. floral scents are blended with sweet romantic notes, woody notes project an aura of sophistication and sensuality.

Know Your Body Type

To determine your body shape you need to consider your height, frame, the widest and the narrowest points of your body and their relationship to each other. Use a full-length mirror to examine your figure. Commence with your shoulder bone and visualize a vertical line running straight down your body from your armpit crease. Now, assess your body shape following the undermentioned table:

BODY SHAPE

Angular: Body appears broader above the waist than below it. Straight, broad sometimes bony shoulders. Rest of the body falling at a rectangular slope to the waist.

Heart: Body is wider above the waist than below it. Upper forearms wider than the shoulders with the bust coming close to or over hanging the imaginary line (mentioned above).

Pear: Body hangs over the imaginary line below the waist and the upper part of the body stays inside the imaginary line.

Curvy pear: Thighs and hips hang over equally.

Straight pear: Thighs hang over more than the hips.

Ellipse: Body runs parallel with the imaginary line from the bust area down to hips and then slopes towards a slimmer thigh area.

Curvy ellipse: Waist hangs over the imaginary line between the bust and the hip area thereby resulting in very little or no waistline.

Straight ellipse: Shoulders narrower than the waist resulting in waist seem high or nonexistent.

Hourglass balanced: Slim waistline irrespective of the proportionately curvy area below and above the waist. Body may hang over the imaginary line at the bust and hips.

Curvy: Extra weight accumulates across the bust upper forearms waist and the hips.

Straight: without a waist Balanced shape above and below the waist and in line all the way down the imaginary line.

With a Waist: Narrow-boned and rectangular or broader and squarer body profile.

Knowing your body balance

You can find out how balanced or in proportion your body is, by looking at where certain points fall in relation to your height. The ideal is when your waist falls halfway between your shoulder line and your bottom. If your waist is higher than the midpoint, you are short-waisted. If lower, you're long-waisted.

Undoubtedly a balanced figure looks pleasing to one's eyes but for those who don't have a balanced figure there are ways in which an illusion of balance can be created. To be able to do this, you need to understand the concept of "Line". The term refers to the outline of a up. A line will lead the eye and can be used to create an optical illusion. Following are the tips to balance a short waist:

- Wear a belt which is the same colour as your top.
- Choose a coloured top which you can blouse over a contrasting bottom giving the impression of a lower waist line.
- Choose dresses with tapered skirts, with either a drop-waisted style or no waist detail.

To balance a long waist

- Wear a belt of the same colour as your skirt or trousers.
- Choose designs that give the illusion of a higher waist, such as skirts with broad waistlines.
- Choose designs that miss the waist and emphasize other parts of the body.

Body shape and balance of body

Here are some guidelines for using both line and colour to great effect for each figure type:

HEART TYPE

- Shoulder pads allow the fabric to hang free and clear of the wider part of the arm.
- For wide waist and trunk use a slightly looser style line.
- Centre detail and cut-in sleeves divide your upper body making it look smaller visually.
- A dress with shoulder pads, creative button placement and the centre detail provided by the heart-shaped neckline all take the eye from the heavy forearms and balance the heart-shaped figure.

STRAIGHT TYPE

- Shoulder pads can be used to balance a tunic or dress in semi-fitted A-line kurtas.
- A dress with shoulder pads, short sleeves and horizontal pockets (if you want) gives width to the top half of the body making the waist, hips and things look smaller and more shapely.
- For a broad straight figure the clever use of colour in patterns can focus attention on selected areas of the body as well as making it look slimmer.

ANGULAR TYPE

- A low-yoke design with sleeves and yoke picked out in a non-advancing colour will take the focus away from the shoulders.
- An unusual line-design features and fabric mixes can focus the eye to the centre, away from the broad shoulder.

PEAR TYPE

- Use of shoulder pads and a light colour on the top half will visually give you more width and will make your waist appear smaller.
- Wearing dark and subdued colours on the bottom half will minimize your thigh area.
- A dress with a low, curved, dropped waist is another good choice as this emphasizes your smooth waistline.
- Perhaps a white dress with black background leads the eye away from the thicker areas of the thigh. The white in the jacket may be expansive making the top half of the body look wider thereby creating a balance.
- Cut away jackets break up the horizontal line and give length to the bottom half.

ELLIPSE TYPE

- Choose a dress with yoke to create width, centred buttons for interest.
- Use shoulder pads and line design, to bypass your waist and to emphasize your well shaped thighs and hips.
- Straight ellipse figure may put on a plain and patterned fabrics worked together.
- Whereas a curvy ellipse figure could wear the above mentioned by reversing the fabrics.

HOURGLASS TYPE

- Dress with sleeves and outside panels in a non-advancing colour and centre panels in an advancing colour would suit this figure type the most.
- Semi-fitted dress with shoulder pads gives smooth emphasis to the waist and the thighs.
- The dark coloured for the bottom half balances a heavy bottom particularly the colour worn on the bottom half is incorporated into the top half.

Fashion and You

Everyone, regardless of size, can develop a personal style that makes the most of their positive features and minimizes the negative ones. All you need to do is to keep the following in view

Average figure

- Always match or tone shoe and hose colours to your hemline colour to lengthen your legs.
- Select neutral and basic colours for business wear.
- A short or long coat can add a contrasting colour effect.
- Wear colours which are close in colour value that is, wearing a single colour from head to foot. Match shoe and hose colours to outside and/or inside garment colours.

- A contrasting jacket should finish in the area between your natural waist and above your full hip.
- Avoid hemline patterns and frills or any straight horizontal lines from the hipline downwards.
- Avoid overwhelming details such as extra large collars and belts; over sized sleeves; big bold prints; bulky fabric; too many collar breaks; excessive fullness and garments that are too long.

Short, broad figure

- Wear a single colour from head to toe or add a contrasting colour at the neckline. For instance if you're wearing a sari with lot of blue you should choose blue for your blouse too. Suits should be of a single colour.

- Keeping shoes, hose and dress in the same colour, add another colour in your jacket, cardigan or coat.
- Keeping shoes, hose, skirt and jacket in one of your best neutral colours, a multicoloured blouse in a lightweight fabric in your best basic colour.
- To look taller and narrower, avoid fitted curvy lines, too much fullness, too many details, large fussy sleeves, horizontal stripes, heavy-looking fabrics and over use of colour breaks which create straight, horizontal lines.
- Go in for suit designs that taper towards the bottom. A lot of pleats and flounce will make you look fatter and wider.
- Select fabrics with tiny prints, flowers or designs.
- Avoid heavy or wide bordered saris. A thin border is the best. Same goes for *pallus* too.
- Do not wear blouses with a gather at the arms. Also avoid tight fitting suits. They will show off the bulk.
- Wear high heels.

Tall, thin figure

- Use shoulder pads to help create a waist.
- Though heavy fabric for skirts can add width to your body, but mind you, this can overwhelm your boney structure thus making your legs and arms look thinner.
- Add a built to pick up the colour of your skirt or blouse to create break.
- To create interest at the neck area, use a contrasting colour for a collar or deep yoke.
- Avoid straight, vertical lines, a monolook, clingly designs and fabric.
- Horizontal stripes in saris or dresses give the appearance of fullness.
- Straight hemlines add width to the body.
- Brightly patterned dresses and saris will give you some fullness.
- Kurtas should be full with a lot of gathers. A skirt type kurta with a wide belt would look very good on you.

Tall, broad figure

- Select designs with vertical lines, or lines that close asymmetrically. These have a slimming effect and create interest.
- Choose loose-fitting, semi-fitted or flared garments.
- Break up vertical lines on the top half of the body by wearing more than one colour.
- Pick out one of the darker or more subdued colours from your top and use it as a block colour for your bottom half.
- Choose a one-piece dress with a big collar in a contrasting colour which extends down the middle.
- Use deep yokes, provided your bust line can stand them.
- Use diagonal and asymmetrical lines with two-tone colouring.
- Wear elasticated waistbands for comfort.
- Avoid clingy fabrics, fussy sleeves, horizontal stripes and short jackets.
- Also avoid lines that are too curved or have too much fullness, and small design details which appear out of proportion.
- Balance head size with a soft medium-volume hairstyle.
- Wear designs that have vertical lines. There designs will create the illusion of thinness. Horizontal stripes on the contrary make you look more rounded and heavier.

- Don't wear large prints or pastel shades. These will only make you look fatter.
- When you wear dresses, go in for A-line cuts. These will make a person look taller and take the attention away from the figure.
- Dark shades should be worn more than light or pastel shades. The best colours are black, navy blue, bottle green, brown, rust etc.
- If your upper arms are very heavy, avoid sleeveless blouses. They will focus attention on the rolling fat.
- Two colour suits, with the kurta in a darker colour will also help.
- When you buy or make suits, avoid patterns with lot of *kalis*, which add to the bulk. Simple straight cuts should be preferred.
- If you want to take away attention from your heavy hips, do not pin the sari up. Instead, leave the *pallu* loose, flowing over your left arm.
- Wear fabrics which do not stand away from the body, like organza, organdy etc. When you wear cotton, starch the garments mildly. They will cling closer to the body.
- Jewellery should not be large, heavy or chunky. A single strand of small pearls, a thin golden chain with a small pendant, or a couple of long chains of gold will look good. Avoid chunky necklaces,
- Wear several thin bangles instead of one heavy *kada*.
- Rings in the ears will make your face look thinner.
- If your face is large and fleshy, avoid huge bindis. Either reduce the size of the round bindis or go in for the various fancy shapes that are vertical in design.

Colour Aesthetics and You

Most people can choose a simple colour that looks good on them, but few of us can combine colours that make us look especially attractive, or choose colours that are appropriate for our life style. Like other swift changes in life our likes and dislikes, norms and values about the use of colours have undergone a drastic change.

The colour one unconsciously chooses to wear are vital clues of one"s inner personality and can help one discover oneself. Colours have personalities too, and knowing what they're helps one to select the right colours for the message someone wants to convey. Always choose colours that feel good on you, and are appropriate for the occasion. For our convenience we divide the colours in two broad categories, viz. advancing and non-advancing. By the former we mean the ones that seem to advance towards you when you hold your colour wheels up at arms length. Whereas the latter is just the opposite of the former in its approach towards you. To comprehend the "language" of colours we assist you by providing the meanings of the expression displayed by these colours:

Advancing	Non-Advancing
Active	Passive
Analytical	Intuitive
Animated	Quiet
Assertive	Submissive
Direct	Subtle
Dramatic	Reserved

Men
Dressing for work
a) Casual clothes should be clean, pressed and well fitting.
b) Never outdress your boss.
c) Keep a blue blazer and tie in your office for unexpected appointments.

d) Pay attention to your physique and physical appearance.
e) Invest in high quality separates, e.g. double breasted blue blazer over a white buttoned down shirt always looks great.
f) When wearing a bow neck, mock neck, or turtle neck unit shirt with a suit or sport coat it should be tucked into the trouser.
g) When wearing a belt, it should be colour coordinated with the shoes.
h) Trouser length should at least touch the top of your shoe.

Formal wear

a) A blazer teamed with trousers and shirt is ideal for a cocktail party.
b) For dinner, a full shirt with a black tie is ideal.
c) For formal occasions during the day, the nature of the occasion dictates how to dress e.g. a dark suit is the most festive.
d) If one has received an invitation beforehand, dress festively.
e) In case of parties, events at night, dress shirt, e.g. Knighthood teamed with dark trousers and a blazer is most appropriate.
f) An all time outfit for an evening out is a kurta pyjama.

Tie

- The quality of a tie is judged by its fall. Drape the tie across your waist and it falls down as it does from the neck. It should fall down straight without twisting.
- Tie's texture should be smooth to touch.
- Check the back side of the tie for its bar tack which is the short horizontal strip that keeps the two sides of the tie together.

Summer Clothes

The weather does not allow for any other clothes than cotton or cotton-blends. Pure cottons and handloom are the best for the hot humid months of summer. But if you have no time for starching and ironing the cottons, you can go in for blends of cotton where, synthetic content keeps the fabric from getting crushed as much as pure cottons. Even if they do, all you may need to do is iron the dresses lightly. These dresses and saris have the advantage of being cool and elegant too.

Children will be happy wearing cotton T-shirts, frocks and skirts. Or maybe Bermudas (loose half-pants) and a coloured vest.

- Get them cotton socks to be worn under their sneakers. These absorb perspiration and prevent rashes.
- Generally buy dresses that are loose fitting since tight fitting ones can be hot and uncomfortable.
- Go in for light shades since dark shades absorb heat.
- Avoid wearing shoes if you can. Wear sandals or chappals instead. Where the dress code of the office demands that you wear shoes, wear cotton socks. Let children wear open sandals that let their feet breathe.
- Keep aside your heavy silks and brocades for the summer months.
- The make-up should also be light. Too much of foundation and creams will make you sweat inside them and ruin your skin.

Winter

Winter clothes consists of sweaters, shawls, warm underclothes and coats. Children need more than a few sweaters since they get them dirty very fast. These should preferably be in darker shades since lighter shades show up dirt.

These are the basic winter clothes you need to buy:

- A pair of woollen socks/stockings.
- A couple of warm banians/chemise and pyjamas.
- At least two sweaters for daily use and one or two for outings.
- A couple of shawls at least. You can buy more to match with your dresses, if you so desire.
- If you have to bear severe winters, go in for an overcoat. When you are at home, you can wear kurtas or housecoats made of warm materials like flannel or wool.
- One firan made of wool.
- One woollen or silk scarf.
- If you go out very often or drive a vehicle then you must have a pair of gloves.

You need not have a dozen shawls or sweaters to match every sari or salwar suit. Buy one or two in neutral colours like maroon, off-white, brown or grey. These colours go well with other colours. For special occasions you can have matching shawls and sweaters.

Tips for buying clothes

- Avoid buying clothes off the pavement stalls since the quality is quite bad. Even though you may feel you are saving money, you will end up spending more since the colour may run or the fabric may lose shape or even tear. You may say that not all clothes are like that. But it is very difficult to make out the good from the bad.
- Watch out for sales in well known stores. Every shop has a clearance sale just before a season sets in or at the end of the season. In direct company sales or factory sales, the stock is fresh and can be safely bought.
- Another event you can look out for, is the "seconds" sale of reputed mills. However, look very minutely for the flaws in the fabric before buying. Sometimes it may be an irregular print that can be hidden in the folds of the sari or an unprinted section that can be cut and discarded while stitching the garment.
- When you buy readymade clothes, look out for the fabric, the stitching, the other trimmings used and colour fastness. It is a good idea to reinforce the stitching by putting a second stitch either over the original one or very close to it. Also secure hooks, buttons, etc.
- When you buy a sari, buy two blouse pieces of different shades. This not only gives a different look to the same sari, but also prevents one blouse from going dull if used alone.

A word about accessories

- The belt should never be so wide or tight that it pulls in the flesh, causing a bulge above and below.
- The shorter the skirt, the narrower the belt and vice-versa.
- If you want to wear a belt but do not want to draw attention to your waist wear it loose with an unbuttoned jacket or cardigan, allowing just a small part of the belt either side of the buckle to be seen.
- Before adding a handbag, briefcase etc. to your look ask yourself what look you're trying to achieve.

- A scarf can give a favourite old garment a more fashionable look.
- Also a scarf can lift, tone or change the look of a garment colour.

Some handy dressing tips

- Avoid wearing dark colours, especially midnight blue or black during an afternoon party or celebration. Reserve these for the nights.
- Dress your forehead with some of the exotic and beautiful bindi available in the market. They can liven up your dress.
- Many women wear their party dress while going to work if they have to attend a party after office. This may be inconvenient and crush the dress by evening. To avoid this, keep a change of blouse—preferably a dressy one that can go with the sari you are wearing. Take some costume jewellery along. Change in the evening for a jazzed up look. To complete the party look, open out your hair and give it a good brushing, apply some make-up and you are all set for the party!
- Avoid wearing dresses made of flimsy stuff in the rainy season. Because if you happen to get wet then they get dressed very soon and make you feel uneasy. Some clothes require lining and if they don't have one, don't forget to wear a chemise inside.
- Always keep safety pins with you, so that whenever, if at all, stitches go undone you can use a safety pin right then and thus can avoid an embarrassing situation.
- In the summers try to wear cotton dresses because they are climate friendly for Indian conditions further they help you soak sweat, keep you free of rashes. If you wear a dress with lining that is an obvious choice for summers.
- If being a working woman you are hard pressed for time, choose saris of drip-dry materials or of the material which as far as possible is crease resistant, non-ironing type.
- While buying saris always check the length and width and never buy a sari which's less than 5 metres.
- When choosing a sari never pick the one which"s been displayed in the shop because constant exposure to light makes such pieces faded and almost lustre less. So ask for the fresh one.
- Don't show off your preference for any dress, no matter how much do you like that particular piece. Because judging your weakness the shopkeeper might quote a higher price.

Short, broad figure

- Wear a sari with small prints, narrow borders and vertical stripes.
- Avoid wearing sari or salwar suits with a pattern of horizontal strips and try to wear footwears with some heel.
- Also avoid too many pleats around the waist, and starch in clothes which add to the width.
- Preferably wear prints which are small in pattern and have vertical stripes.
- If you are going to wear salwar suits remember not to wear a very long kurta. Kurta should be near or just below the knees. If possible wear salwar with vertical stripes.
- While wearing sari tie it above the navel to give the lower part of your body a length.
- Don't wear very dark colours.

- Wear dresses made of the stuff which have good fall e.g. chiffon, wrinkled cotton.

Tall, thin figure

- Wear the dresses which add width to your body—like organdy, organza, tissue, tusser silk etc.
- Wear long kurta with some zig-zag patterned stripes on it, while wearing sari tie it below the navel.
- Avoid wearing heels.
- Wear dark and bright colours.
- If possible wear well starched clothes.
- Preferably avoid wearing churidar pajamas and tight jeans in particular and well-fitting dresses in general.
- Avoid wearing stuff which clings to the body.
- Wear saris with bold prints, big skirt borders and horizontal design because these will enhance your look.

Tall, broad figure

- Tie your sari just on where your navel is so that you can balance your stature.
- Break the colouring of your dress, that is, preferably avoid wearing single coloured or patterned dress. Wear contrast and combination.
- Avoid wearing very bright colours.

Chiffon

Chiffon saris are light and lovely - ideal for the hot, summer evenings. French chiffon saris are difficult to get these days, so look after yours carefully to make them last. Chiffon saris are now being manufactured in India and some of them are very attractive.

Never try to wash chiffon at home. Always send your chiffon garments to a reliable dry cleaner.

Chin

If you have a large or prominent chin, or if your chin is too "weak" you can disguise the defect with the clever use of cosmetics (see cosmetic modelling).

If a double chin is your problem, you can banish it by doing these exercises every day, and by sleeping without a pillow:

Exercise 1: Sitting in an upright position, bend your head back as far as it will go, then bring it slowly back to position. Repeat five times, gradually increasing to ten.

Exercise 2: Sitting at a table, rest your elbows on the table top and slap the fat under your chin with the backs of your hands.

Cholis

Since your choli is the garment nearest your face, do choose yours in colours that flatter your complexion.

Here are a few hints to help you choose the choli style that's most becoming to you:

Neckline: A high neckline covers up scrawny shoulders, but should never be worn by someone with a short neck. A V-neckline makes a stubby neck look longer. A wide "off-the-shoulder" neckline should only be worn by someone with pretty shoulders.

Sleeves: Sleeveless cholis are suitable for short girls, as they give the impression of added height. They may also be worn with good effect to show off pretty arms. Sleeves ending just above the elbows are most flattering to women with plump arms. Little cap sleeves, ending an inch or two below the shoulder are suitable for young girls and women with slender arms.

Length: The length of cholis seems to be getting shorter and shorter! While it's fashionable to display a wide strip of bare midriff, it is better to keep the choli slightly longer unless you are very slim because a "spare tyre" bulging out beneath a short choli looks very ugly.

To spark off your own creative ideas about good combinations for salwar-kamiz here are some suggestions to build on:

For morning wear

1. White churidars, blue and white paistry patterned kurta, matching blue dupatta.
2. Pale yellow salwar, printed kamiz in shades of yellow, green and white. Dupatta made from the same printed material.
3. Pale pink churidars, checked gingham kurta in pale grey and white with pink embroidery around the sleeves and neckline.

For afternoon wear

1. Cyclamen churidars. Slim, full sleeved kamiz, richly printed in shades of cyclamen, green and slate. Green dupatta.

2. A bold, burnt orange and black kamiz, teamed with black churidars and dupatta.
3. Pale coffee churidars and kurta with elaborate embroidery in leaf green and white all around the yoke and sleeves. Pale coffee dupatta.

For evening wear

1. Copper coloured satin churidars. Natural raw silk kamiz with zari embroidery work around the neckline.
   Old gold dupatta in fine chiffon.
2. Black silk churidars. Mandarin-style kamiz in white, black and red. White dupatta.
3. White satin salwar. White silk kamiz with silver zari butis. White dupatta sprinkled with tiny silver sequines.

Sari

Saris are the most beautiful and graceful of all garments. They suit all women and cover up a multitude of figure faults. So give the sari its due by wearing it well.

1. Tuck in the inside edge of your sari, taking care to see that the length is correct. About 1" from floor level is the right length (nothing looks worse than an ankle-high sari) If you are going to wear high heels, put on your sandals before tying the sari, as your heels can make quite a lot of difference to how long your sari will look.
2. Tuck in firmly, all the way round, gathering it up a little in the centre back, so that the fabric will not "seat".
3. Take the pallu across the back and place it on the left shoulder to the desired length. The length may be:
   (a) Very short—known as the "duster" style in which the pallu is only about

12" long. (In this case the sari should be tightly draped across the front, tracked into the waist at the back, and then placed over the arm.)

(b) Average length—this is worn hip length and is the most usual length, as well as being the most practical for everyday wear.

(c) Full length—here the pallav is worn long and flowing, until it almost touches the floor. This looks very elegant and is suitable for formal evening wear.

4. Take the remaining material to form the front pleats. Starting from the right, first make a broad, deep pleat about 5" wide. Then go on making pleats about 3" wide until all the material has been pleated.

5. Holding the pleats tightly together, neaten them out, pressing them firmly to keep them in place. Now tuck in the pleats, taking care to see that the edge of the sari is 1" from the floor. When tucking in the pleats, see that they lie flatly and neatly under the petticoat so that they will not look bulky.

6. Finally, drape the pallav neatly across the front and over the arm.

Jewellery

There is nothing to beat the charm of gold, pearls or diamonds when it comes to jewellery. These can be either simple or elaborate, delicate or chunky, depending upon the occasion.

A simple strand of pearls combined with delicate chiffon gives a grand appearance. Likewise a diamond jewellery set looks stunning with a heavy silk sari. Take care though not to look like a jewellery stand, wearing a lot of them.

With the fear of robberies and chain snatching on the rise, costume jewellery is getting to be very popular. These come in a wide range of materials and designs and can go with any dress and be suitable for every occasion. The best thing about costume jewellery is that they come in a variety of colours to match your dress. Moreover, they are inexpensive and therefore you can have several sets to go with various dresses. American diamond is another inexpensive substitute for real diamonds. Anyway most women keep diamonds safely in their lockers to avoid theft.

Care of pearls

- Keep pearls in a separate pouch to protect them from being scratched.
- Don't let pearls rub together.
- Take care to ensure that the pearls are not crushed.
- Don't wear your pearls when they might be splashed with ammonia, ink, vinegar or acids that can damage them.
- To clean pearls, wipe them with a cloth moistened with mild soap and water.
- Rinse, then dry the pearls with a soft cloth. Never use jewellery cleaner on pearls.
- Have pearls restrung regularly.

Gold

- To clean gold at home use soapnuts (ritha).
- Beware of vendors who come home and offer to clean your gold.
- These people have special chemicals which help them steal gold while cleaning.

Silver

- Wash the item in warm soapy water.
- Polish with silver polish and a soft cloth.

- Store in a dark place.
- Exposure to humidity and sunlight causes metal to tarnish.
- Silver zari work can be polished by a dry cleaner.

Diamonds: while selecting diamonds one should remember

- Go to an experienced and trusted jeweller.
- The quality and size of the stone determines its value.
- Diamonds should be set in platinum.
- The worth of diamond depends on 4 Cs.
- i) **Colour:** The best colour is colourless. However, they may be of several colours including blue.
- ii) **Cut:** A good cut is what gives a diamond its sparkle and fire. A well cut diamond usually has 58 cuts.
- iii) **Carat weight:** A carat is divided into 100 points so that a diamond of 25 points is described as quiquarter of a carat or .25 carats.
- iv) **Clarity:** refers to the diamond's purity. Some black spots known as nature's vinglipunts are found in the diamonds. The fewer such spots, the more valuable the stone because the flow of light is less obstructed.

Handy hints

- Do not wear very heavy jewellery or diamonds during the day. They look better in the evenings.
- Sometimes wearing just a thin chain of gold around your neck will make you look more stunning than loading up on jewels, especially if you are wearing a simple chiffon or silk.
- A thumb of rule is to avoid loads of jewellery, especially if they clash. For example, a ruby necklace will look awful with an emerald pendant. Pearls worn with diamonds will be a real disaster.

Handbags and footwear

These are as much accessories, as part of your personality. So be careful while choosing a handbag.

- Have at least a couple of roomy handbags with a lot of storage space for your daily office use. You can alternate them. Keep them large because you never know if you will need to pick up something on the way home from work—a kilo of apples, a packet of tea or maybe the painting box that your son wanted.
- However, if you believe in keeping home and office separate, carry a nylon shopping bag, folded, in your handbag!
- While buying a bag, remember to go in for usefulness rather than just appearance. A narrow-necked bag may look beautiful in the shop but may not accommodate your folder or lunch box. It would be better to invest in a single leather bag that will be sturdy and look good too. A shoulder slung bag is more convenient especially if you have to hang on to the strap in a crowded bus.
- For parties and other special occasions, you can carry a small purse or sling bag, in which you can keep your powder compact, lipstick and comb or even your make-up kit.
- Shoulder-slung briefcases are both sleek and sophisticated. If you have files and folders or lots of paper, go in for one

of these. The advantage is that, you can even carry it like a briefcase.
- Denim and suede are both sturdy and sophisticated. You can buy good handbags in one of these materials.

Footwear

Footwear should be comfortable and easy to walk on. This is more important if you are going to be on your feet all day at work. Unless they are comfortable, you will end up with a bad strain on your legs. For daily use, go in for simple footwear—sandals that buckle up or chappals that are soft and flat. As a rule, avoid wearing stilettos to work if you have a lot of walking to do. Anything more than a two-inch heel would be uncomfortable when you have to wear it the whole day.

Slip-on shoes (bally) are most comfortable and can be worn with any dress—be it a sari or salwar-kameez suit. These are available in leather, suede and canvas, and come in a wide variety of colours and designs. If you wear jeans and shirt to work, you can wear sneakers (sports shoes). They are very comfortable on the feet.

Very high heels are fashionable, but are not good for your back. If you have any problem with your back, avoid wearing high heels. Pregnant women should strictly avoid high heels.

■■

SELF-HELP/PERSONALITY DEVELOPMENT
(आत्म-सुधार/व्यक्तित्व विकास)

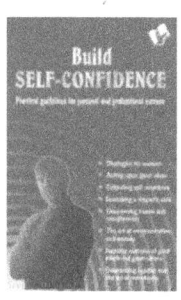

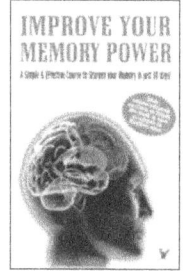

Contact us at sales@vspublishers.com

SELF IMPROVEMENT (आत्म विकास) | ENGLISH IMPROVEMENT (अंग्रेजी सुधार)

STRESS MANAGEMENT (तनाव मुक्ति)

All books available at www.vspublishers.com

CAREER & BUSINESS MANAGEMENT
(कॅरियर एण्ड बिजनेस मैनेजमेंट)

JOB RELATED
(नौकरी सम्बन्धी)

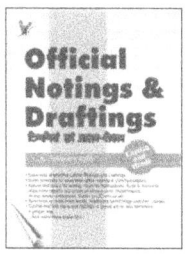

Contact us at sales@vspublishers.com

STUDENT DEVELOPMENT/LEARNING
(छात्र विकास/लर्निंग)

JOKES
(हास्य)

MAGIC & FACT (जादू एवं तथ्य)

MUSIC (संगीत)

COMPUTER

All books available at www.vspublishers.com

www.ingramcontent.com/pod-product-compliance
Lightning Source LLC
Chambersburg PA
CBHW081909110426
R18126400001B/R181264PG42743CBX00007B/1